JOURNEY
INTO
JOY

Arthur H. De Kruyter

JOURNEY INTO JOY

Guideposts

CARMEL • NEW YORK 10512

This Guideposts edition is published by special arrangement with Fleming H. Revell Company

Library of Congress Cataloging in Publication Data

DeKruyter, Arthur H.
  Journey into joy.

  1. Spirituality. 2. Christian life—1960–
I. Title.
BV4501.2.D433   1985   248.4   84-11504
ISBN 0-8007-1219-6

Contents

Part IV: Journey Into Divine Power   **149**

INTRODUCTION
Beginning Your Spiritual Pilgrimage

Imagine yourself about to begin the most exciting journey of your life. The days when your main role in life was that of a businessman, homemaker, student or wage earner are about to end. You slip off into a different world, populated with powerful friends and supernatural enemies.

There will be days of unspeakable joy, times of hardship, and countless adventures. Occasionally you will feel weary and confused, but through it all, you will experience the deep satisfaction of knowing God is on your side. At other times great mysteries will become clear to you and impossible dreams will come true.

You become a stronger, better person as the journey progresses. As iron sharpens iron, encounters along the way add to your personality. You become more sensitive and loving. Those around you see a new warmth in your smile and sparkle in your eyes.

The journey I am describing in figurative language is very real to some Christians, who fully realize that when they com-

mitted their hearts to Jesus Christ they embarked on a spiritual
journey that would last the rest of their lives. These happy
Christians realize our lives are not just spent in time and space,
but in the realm of the spirit: "For our struggle is not against
flesh and blood," Paul writes in Ephesians 6:12 (NIV), "but
against . . . the powers of this dark world and against the spiritual forces of evil. . . ."

Growing in spirituality is as much an adventure as Odys-
seus's experiences on strange islands, his struggles against unknown powers, or his battles against monsters. We wrestle with
spiritual forces. With God beside us, we grit our teeth and slog
along through the Slough of Despond, or we raise our voices in
shouts of triumph as the Giant Despair is overcome.

Despite the hardships of this venture, it provides opportunities to draw closer to God. The benefits far outweigh the trials
in this journey into joy. As the believer travels, he develops
both mind and heart in loving God, combining knowledge and
experience.

The process of reaching greater spirituality never ends—new
insights always remain just ahead as we walk life's pathway.
The pursuit of godliness is a rich and intensely personal process beginning with a relationship with God through Jesus
Christ.

A very wise man set out to achieve a full understanding of
God and his creation. He began his ambitious project with
great energy, and for years and years he persevered. He studied
books, traveled around the world to interview holy men, spent
months in reflective thought, and wrestled with religious problems far beyond the understanding of common people. He
lived to a ripe old age. On his deathbed, someone asked him
about his achievements.

"Wise man," the visitor asked, "do you understand God?"

"I am like a child sitting on a beach," the old man said. "All
my life I have contemplated grains of sand. I have seen thousands of them, and now at the end of my life I have filled a little pail with sand from the beach. But there is a whole beach
full of grains of sand that I could not even touch in a thousand

lifetimes. That is how great God is. His riches are beyond understanding. We can spend a lifetime exploring just tiny portions of his creation."

My Own Experience

In the last few years I have made the exciting discovery that a life of spirituality requires not simply mastering doctrine, understanding theology, or memorizing Scripture. The spiritual life goes beyond the intellect. It meshes understanding with feeling. When analytical knowledge of God is balanced with feelings inspired by God, then we can enjoy a full, rich relationship with Jesus Christ.

It has taken me years to find this out. I want to share my experience with you so you may make the same kind of journey to a deeper level of spiritual reality in your own life.

I come from a religious family. At age eight, I began to attend catechism classes once a week. This was in addition to attending worship services twice each Sunday and church-school classes every Sunday morning. I rarely missed a church service or instructional class. I attended a Christian elementary school, and later I attended a Christian high school, a Christian college, and two different seminaries.

At age seventeen I appeared before the elders in my church to make a public Christian commitment. In our church, we called such an act a "confession of faith." With my head packed full of religious knowledge, I stood up in front of the elders and submitted myself to probing questions. The minister excused himself when the questioning began and quickly went next door to the parsonage to retrieve his personal copy of the catechism book. In the presence of the elders, he then asked me more than a hundred questions.

I was able to give him all the answers he sought in a proper and systematic manner. At the conclusion of that interview, I was asked to leave the room while the elders and the pastor discussed my "confession." A few minutes later they informed me that in their judgment I was a Christian and I could stand in the presence of the congregation and testify to my faith in Jesus.

In seminary, I had a meticulous professor who taught his students the discipline of thorough sermon preparation. His emphasis was on the discovery of the theme of a scriptural passage, followed by a sequence of logical statements developing and expanding that theme. My classmates and I would rake through commentaries and use every tool of Bible research at our disposal to try to please the professor. But I remember only one occasion in the three years that anyone came close to reaching his high standards for applying that sermon preparation technique. Unfortunately, that individual was not me!

According to my professor, a foolproof method would unlock the inevitable logic of the Scripture. For more than three decades, I wrestled with a conscience born of my professor's indelible impression. But while being true to Scripture, my sermons lacked an indefinable something that could reach not only the head, but the heart of my congregation. My Christianity was based on the analysis of truth. It was a way of looking at life, a sort of Christian philosophy. I sensed that something was missing, yet for many years I was unable to put my finger on it.

At the conclusion of my studies at the second seminary, I was examined by the seminary faculty and two review boards within my church. They questioned me on the facts of my Christian faith, including church history, doctrine, ethics, and Bible knowledge.

I passed these examinations and offered a brief statement of my personal commitment to serve Jesus Christ as a faithful custodian of the truth of the Word of God.

Then I was admitted into the ministry. For many years since, I have preached the truths of the Bible. It never occurred to me that there was more to the Christian life than a thorough understanding of the Christian faith and consistent obedience. Propositional truth meant everything to me. I can honestly say that I enjoyed its logic. I have always had personal organizational skills, and putting everything into a neat, clean system appealed to me.

While my ministry went along successfully toward its goal of reaching people with God's truth, I uncomfortably felt something was missing. A piece of the puzzle still eluded me. This unrest prompted me to continue to pursue whatever it was that could complete the picture.

While I was on this personal journey, similar feelings were stirring in many other Christians in other circles besides my own. An element of Christianity began to emphasize feelings or emotions. Within highly structured ecclesiastical bodies in America, I saw a growing desire for religious experience that incorporated emotions more integrally with spiritual growth. My recognition of this new emphasis led me to raise questions about the validity of the way I was handling my ministry.

From my counseling experience, as well as my personal spiritual life, I found that the emotions and the feelings play a major role in determining what happens in the life of an individual. It finally dawned on me that some of the greatest decisions in life are not made solely on the basis of intellectual understanding; feelings play a very important role as well. In fact, in many if not most decisions, feelings play the dominant role.

We do not marry because of analysis. Nor do we choose a vocation because of a computerized evaluation of alternatives. Rather we are attracted to a person or to our life's work because of a relationship that the mind alone cannot always define. This is true in my own life. I chose the ministry because of my private, personal relationship with God. And during my ministry, I have sought to deepen that.

Through all this I learned that the idea of giving greater play to feelings and emotions in the Christian life was not a new phenomenon. What I was beginning to understand and what other pastors and laymen were pondering was not new at all.

The desire for a relationship with God that could include feelings and emotions as well as logic and analysis has been going on ever since the church began. I began to read everything I could find on the topic. Almost to my surprise, I discovered that there were *feelings* and *experiences* associated with prayer, meditation, love, joy, healing, and worship that I didn't really understand. Things were going on in the area of Christian spirituality that I didn't know how to handle. My personal search led me to Christians who would help me understand these things.

One day a friend pointed me in the direction of Spain. He told me about Christians there who were in touch with a body of material produced in the sixteenth century, mainly by a woman known as Sister Teresa of Avila and a man now known as Saint John of the Cross. Although these two people had written down their thoughts hundreds of years ago, their work was supposed to have ramifications for spiritually sensitive Christians of the modern world.

The conference in Spain became a turning point in my life. I left Chicago, Illinois, an international hub of commerce and industry, and I found myself in a world shaped by different religious thought, different cultural patterns, and historical events that had occurred centuries before my own country even existed. Life moved at a different pace. No automobiles were allowed in the central part of the city, called the plaza, and on the warm nights families would walk slowly over the cobblestones, chatting and laughing. I stayed with my wife in a university room that held little more than a bed, table, light-bulb, and two chairs. Insects occasionally drifted into the room through unscreened windows.

My mornings and evenings were spent in classrooms, and afternoons I devoted to reading. From the priests who led the conference, I learned that in the Catholic Church there exists a body of information that recognizes emotions and feelings in the practice of faith. Carefully written documents described ways of building a personal, experiential relationship with God. Sister Teresa and Saint John had discovered ways to organize the Christian life around the basic disciplines of prayer, meditation, solitude, simplicity, and other aspects of spirituality. They not only described these disciplines, but they recounted ways of developing them in a Christian's life.

The work of Sister Teresa had been done at a time when many convents in Spain had been riddled with corruption. The church of her day was losing the desire to pray, meditate, and worship. This nun was a doer, not a thinker. She spoke. She worked quietly. She won the hearts of the common people. She learned spiritual truths and put them into practice.

Saint John of the Cross was another dedicated Christian who found himself in the midst of corruption. He recognized in the life of Sister Teresa important qualities that should be shared with other Christians. The priest supported her efforts to find true spirituality and provided her with theological backing when anyone questioned her practices. Together these dedicated Christians tested their findings against the Scriptures, and they strove always for spiritual integrity in their actions.

Sister Teresa made a deep impression on people around her in the convents, and word of her actions and thoughts spread to Rome. It was just a matter of time before the church asked her to commit to writing the things she was doing and the lessons she had learned. At first she felt reluctant to do so, but she eventually produced a body of written material. Her journey of the heart was reduced to writing.

In a sense, Sister Teresa and Saint John of the Cross sought to reform the Catholic Church from within. In a limited way, they actually accomplished something like a reformation. Everything they accomplished, however, was lost in the sweep of history. In the fury of the Inquisition and the drive to retain its historic identity, the Church of Spain was not long affected by the work of the quiet nun. Today, in fact, only a limited number of Christians know anything about it.

Another strong-willed, passionate, eloquent, fiercely dedicated Christian had occupied center stage in Europe earlier in the century in which Sister Teresa explored spirituality: Martin

Luther. Today, whenever the word *Reformation* is used, our thoughts go immediately to Luther and the theses on the door of the Castle Church of Wittenberg.

You know the story of the European Reformation. Let me recount just a few facts about it to compare it to the quiet reformation in Spain. Luther felt that the church had failed to maintain the integrity of its theology. He drove the church to rethink a number of doctrinal issues. His concern was that the church present the Scriptures as the guide and authority for believers. He descried the conflict between some of the church's practices and biblical truth.

In a sense, Luther was not looking for something new from the church. Rather he called upon the church to consider once again the truth which it already confessed. Martin Luther brought knowledge of the system and of the Scriptures to the attention of the people. The Protestant Reformation was born out of that intellectual struggle.

Ever since that time, those of us in the Protestant Church have been aware of the need for systematic study of and loyalty to Scripture. We have organized, studied, labeled, and systematized our theology.

Two Reformations Compared

The Reformation begun by Luther in Germany had entirely different results from the reformation in Spain. Luther was expelled from the church; Sister Teresa and Saint John stayed within the church. The mystics (those who based their spirituality on information not attained through rational theorizing) in Spain renewed and reformed the spiritual disciplines described at various points in Scripture.

Luther challenged the church's theology, while Teresa and John challenged its spirit. One emphasized intellectual truth—the propositional side of faith—the others dealt with the experiential aspect, found in daily renewal of relationships in believers' lives.

Sister Teresa and Saint John found their reformation spontaneous and filled with excitement. It had a private, profound impact in the lives of many. Their reformation renewed the practice of personal spirituality, including the disciplines of prayer, solitude, and meditation.

The German Reformation was intellectual and well organized, aimed at the corporate process of change. By urging the church to change its theology, Luther felt change would ultimately occur in the body of believers. He documented the process in a careful, organized manner.

I share the contrast in approach by Martin Luther and Sister Teresa to help you sense that difference in your own life. What Luther did in his careful study and analysis of the needs for change and growth is vitally important to the course of church history. But what a rich dimension is gained from the reformation of the heart that took place in Spain! The two together encompass the full spectrum of true spirituality. Both dimensions are vitally important. Having one—whether intellectual or spiritual—without the other leaves less than a complete picture or authentic experience of spirituality.

You can imagine the enthusiasm I felt as I began to grasp the power of what I was learning. I could hardly wait to return home to share this new understanding with my friends and church members!

Back at Home

When I returned from Spain I prepared a series of sermons that explored the various dimensions of what I had learned. I called the series "The Marks of Spirituality." Many people in my church responded favorably to the messages, and I received requests for more information.

This book is an outgrowth of those sermons and the subsequent response; I hope it will help you uncover the various aspects of our journey into joy that have been all but forgotten in some quarters of Christendom.

I sincerely hope that you will find this book more than just an abstract account of my experience. *I want the experience to*

become yours, too. As you read these pages, I hope you will
meet God and he will meet you in new and enriching ways.
The deepening of your spiritual life in the midst of a struggling, questioning, and distrusting society can become a life-
changing experience. It can have a major impact on you and
those around you.

In the following chapters, we will begin from the perspective
of you alone with God. We will explore prayer, with the intent
of learning how to free God's resources; we will delve into
meditation, from the angle of learning how to focus on God;
and we will discover solitude, in the hope that you can learn to
remove distractions in your spiritual quest.

There are basic ingredients that go into the process of personal growth. These become Part II of the book. We will examine the idea of self-esteem and your ability to accept God's
creation: yourself. We will look at simplicity as a commitment
to avoid life's complexities and remain on track toward spiritual growth. Then we will explore fasting, or God's secret
weapon, and its impact on your spirituality.

In Part III, we will step back to look at the basics of your
walk with God. These three building blocks each fit together to
add an important dimension to your spirituality. We will look
at how you believe without fear—practicing faith. We will add
the perspective that you find in love and how love really is
practicing God's motivation. A sometimes welcome addition to
our Christian life is joy; this chapter will concentrate on helping you to learn to feel what you already believe.

The fourth section turns your attention to learning how to
draw on God's power. You will explore the somewhat foreign
experience of accepting God's touch through healing. You will
see the role of worship in your spiritual life as you experience
the presence of God in communal life. Finally, you will explore the idea of balance in your spiritual life and the need to
reach beyond analytical truth in the realm of emotion.

In a real sense, this entire book describes balance. The chapters look at a variety of different aspects of spirituality from the
basic to the complex. They offer ideas for growth and insights

from my own experiences. But the key to the book is taking the things you learn and applying them to your daily life. Take what you know and let your heart work on it for a time. Turn your emotions loose and let them work on what you understand. But don't stop there. Unbridling your emotions is only the first step. Once you experience how your feelings play a role in your Christian walk, you must then begin to bring them into balance with knowledge. Too much understanding, at the expense of feelings, shortchanges your spirituality. Too much emotion, at the expense of logic, becomes equally negative. You must find a balance. Bring the two together evenly and you will be well on your way as you continue your journey toward a deeper and richer relationship to Jesus Christ.

I know you share my desire for spiritual growth, or you probably would not have picked up this book and started to read in the first place. If you approach each chapter with a sincere desire to find understanding and application in your own life, you will gain a great deal from your reading. I pray your journey from mind to heart will prove as rich and rewarding as my own. My relationship with God is far richer for having traveled this road.

Now let us begin the journey together.

Part I

Journey Into God's Resources

1

Prayer: Freeing God's Resources

He withdrew into the wilderness and prayed.
Luke 5:16

Imagine that you could learn how to tap into Ultimate Power! No matter who you are or what you do, you could snap your fingers and have at your command the power of the gods. Minor problems would be dismissed in a puff of smoke. Major problems might take an incantation or two, but with suitable thunderclaps and bursts of colored light they, too, would vanish.

Need money? Wham! Bank accounts are full.

Need health? Zing! Pain is gone. Body is strong.

Need peace? Poof! Discord disappears.

Our literature is full of legends of men and women who were able to obtain this kind of power—Beowulf, King Midas, Dr. Faustus, or King Arthur. Our children read Super Hero comics and fall asleep with bedtime stories of genies in bottles.

So I suppose it is very natural that when we begin to think about the supernatural power of prayer, we revert to the wham-zing-poof school of thought. We think of prayer as a magic solution to insurmountable problems. Like Ali Baba, we run into a dead end and begin to shout, "Open sesame," as we look for a doorway. If we could just find the right words, or perhaps if we could just shout loudly enough, God would hear us and open his storehouse of blessings!

It may be true that prayer links us with the power of God, and sometimes God does decide to perform astounding miracles around a person who prays—but the wham-zing-poof school of thought doesn't even come close to a true understanding of prayer.

True prayer means much more than isolated crisis management. It is an ongoing process of drawing near to God. We must not disconnect our devotional life from the routine events we seem to handle very well without divine intervention. A healthy prayer life is nurtured and developed long before our backs are against the wall and in panic we exclaim, "There's nothing left to do but pray!"

Even the most hardened people realize that there is something wrong with coming to God only in times of crisis. They know, deep inside, that God expects more. As a pastor, I find that sensitive Christians also know that and sincerely *want* to know how to approach God through prayer. They desire to understand the Bible. An inner drive to develop a rich, deep prayer life dwells within them. They are prepared to expend time and energy to draw near to God.

"Teach us to pray," was heard on the shores of Galilee two thousand years ago.

"How can I improve my prayer life?" is heard often in my church during Bible studies or counseling sessions.

Experience has taught me that Christians develop this over a period of time, something like the way athletes, musicians, or teachers develop their skills. These people learn their professions through study, practice, and discipline. One of the tragedies of the United States' withdrawal from the 1980 Winter Olympics was the waste of years of dedicated training that our athletes had undergone in order to raise their skills to the highest level. The best teachers you remember from your elementary or high-school years were probably men and women who had honed their skills over many years at the front of a classroom.

Developing a strong devotional life follows the same pattern. Christians explore their relationship with God, study Scripture, and learn the discipline of coming to God regularly. That process takes time.

In the pages you are about to read, I would like to describe some of the tools that have helped my family, my friends, and myself in our struggles to understand true prayer. I am sure that you will benefit from the lessons we have learned, and I hope that these thoughts will also help explode some myths about prayer.

Pray Persistently

Persistence is an important tool for the Christian who wants to have a strong prayer life. This concept, of course, runs counter to the use of prayer as a last resort.

True prayer becomes a daily or even an hourly exercise. A friend of mine started a little consulting business a couple of years ago. During the first months on his own, he needed to spend as much time as possible in his office or with his clients. That was his profitable time. The hours spent in his car driving to or from clients or running errands around town were "down time" as far as he was concerned. He grew to resent the intervals in his car, even though they formed a necessary part of his daily routine.

My friend told me that his time in the car became less frustrating when he began to use it for silent prayer. At first it was just a few minutes of prayer while he drove across a straight, open stretch of Interstate 80. Then as he began to warm to the practice, he did some praying on shorter trips across town to the bank or the post office. The result was a healthier attitude toward his daily routine, an active prayer life, and a constant dialogue with God.

I don't advocate drive-time prayer for everyone, but I do

know that a spiritual principle was operating in my friend's daily life: *Persistence creates a strong prayer life.* Other Christians achieve the same goals by setting aside daily blocks of time for prayer; some spend a few moments in silent prayer before each meal; and others simply pause during a lull in household chores or the office activities to commune with God.

This same persistence characterized Jesus' prayer life. His personal, intense relationship with God, his Father, was based on prayer. In Luke 5:16, we read, "He withdrew into the wilderness and prayed." Prayer was a priority.

Besides setting a personal example, Christ told us several stories about prayer. In the familiar story of the prodigal son he used contrast to make a point.

So often we play the prodigal-son game in our own lives— returning to our heavenly Father when the going gets tough. We often don't make prayer a vital part of our daily lives. Yet we share the belief that God is loving and kind. We know that he will welcome us any time we come to him. We know that we can give him our burdens, our failures, and our loneliness. If we feel downhearted, we turn to God for help. We expect that God will be like the prodigal son's father—he will meet us as we approach him.

Before we have a chance to say a word, he will have his loving arms around us, welcoming us home. Just like the prodigal son, we pour out our hearts, tell of our follies, and confess our shame to our Father. Jesus taught us an important lesson with the prodigal-son story. We learned that the moment the father saw his son approaching he ran to meet him. More important, before the son could even stammer out his mistakes, the father forgave him, put a robe on him, and welcomed him home. You and I have that assurance as we approach God.

You probably still think the story is all very familiar. But let's take it beyond the apparent and explore further. Obviously the prodigal son did *not* practice persistent prayer, but did you ever stop to think about the father he left behind? If he is at all like me, I am sure that he prayed each and every day for his son. The father's persistent prayer may have been the key to the son waking up one day and realizing how far astray his life had gone.

Have you ever asked what happened after the prodigal son was welcomed home by his father? Did the son actually stay at home? Or did he remain home just long enough to amass another fortune and then go off and try life again? Was he just using his father for his own ends? Had he learned a lesson? What do you think?

I firmly believe that the son really had learned a lesson; he had come home to stay. Jesus told the story to show the error of losing that closeness to the father. He told the story to show the persistent prayer of a father for his son. But he also told the story to demonstrate the idea of sonship, helping us to grasp the relationship we can enjoy with our Father in heaven. The prodigal son enjoyed a warm relationship with his father but lost it because of his behavior. When he realized what he had left, and when he knew that he was wrong and wanted to recapture what he had lost, he found that the love and sonship were still there.

How like the prodigal son we are. We move away from God and so often realize, too late, that we have lost an important relationship. Unique to the Christian faith is the unquestioning love that waits for each of us to return. God is always ready to restore us in his love when we approach him, seeking forgiveness, like the prodigal son. Our key to maintaining a closeness to God—and to regaining it when we have lost it—is to pray. Pray persistently.

But prayer alone is not enough. The Holy Spirit intercedes for us. In Romans 8:26, we read that he ". . . intercedes . . . with groanings that cannot be uttered." Because Christ gave his life for our sins, he becomes our advocate before the Father. In the first chapter of John we read that "We became sons of God when we came to him through Jesus Christ." But there is a price. Like the prodigal son who returned to live under his father's roof, with his father's rules and discipline, we too must give up the independence of a distant land. We must put away a life of doing as we please to rejoin God and live by his rules.

This is another part of the lesson that Christ wove into this rich story. We are accountable to him for our lives. This accountability is balanced by his role as our friend. Persistent prayer enables us to relate to Christ and God. He loves us, and we love him.

That love makes it possible for us to come freely to God, through Jesus Christ, knowing that he will listen and hear our prayers. How different from going before someone and having to be convincing or persuasive. Phillips Brooks said it this way, "Prayer is *not* conquering God's reluctance, but taking hold of God's willingness." We come to him because he is waiting for us. He wants to give. There is no need to be persuasive.

Our relationship with God is like the finest father-son or mother-daughter relationship you can bring to mind. It is a rich association. If you have children, you will remember a time when you were sitting in a chair—reading a book or paper or magazine—and your little son or daughter came over and tried to snuggle into the chair next to you. You smiled, put down the book, threw your arms around your child, and said, "Honey, what do you want?" I remember such an experience with my own daughter, Lucette. Her response was something like, "I don't want anything, Daddy. I just want to sit with you." I am sure you recall how special and meaningful that moment was. That special relationship is exactly what you can enjoy with Jesus Christ. He is there for you whenever you call upon him in prayer.

Because of Jesus, we can go to God as a friend. And like a child just wanting to be with a parent, we can go to God in prayer. We don't need a particular reason or to wait for a crisis or a time when the burdens are more than we can carry. Go to God all the time, as you would spend time with a friend. Feel comfortable going to God in prayer. Too many Christians feel guilty when their prayer needs begin to look like grocery lists. They are tempted to lop the least important things off the list and bring only major life events or serious problems to him. They'll pray about cancer but not the flu. They'll pray about financial matters over $1,000, but try to work things out on their own when the price tag is lower. They'll pray about career moves but not bother about asking for strength for the morning's work.

God *wants* to see the whole list! And even when there isn't a long list, he wants us to come to him. Say something like, "Lord, I don't want to ask for specific things right now. I just want to be close to you."

There is comfort in knowing that we can be ourselves with God. We might as well, because he can see into the inner depths of our beings! He knows us as no other person ever will. Even our best friends on earth will never know us as God does. We are so limited by our view of just the outside surface of things that we often forget God sees *everything*.

Besides being a father, God is our *friend.* That kind of relationship is unique and powerful. Think about it for a moment. There is almost as much power in friendship as in the father-child relationship.

The friendships made by the prodigal son were strong and magnetic. They pulled him into a life of extravagance and waste. They ate up his money and spit him out into the pigsty. I have vivid memories of the power of friendship. As a child I seemed to constantly make friends with the naughtiest boys around. By the time I reached the fifth grade, I knew something was wrong. Even at that age, I could see that I was heading for serious trouble, because I couldn't seem to resist these friendships.

My parents had taught me to pray, so I prayed very hard about the situation. After much prayer—and never underestimate your child's ability to pray!—I felt that the solution was for me to get out of my environment altogether. I approached my parents one evening and told them that I felt I had to change schools.

My parents listened to me. There are times in each parent's life when God provides special grace to really listen to a child and understand the full impact of what he or she is saying. This must have been one of those times, because they listened and *heard* what I was saying. I told them that I had prayed about the problems I was having, and I thought I could make a fresh start in another school near my home. They agreed to my plan.

We talked again that night about being careful when I chose my friends. My parents shared their concern that I choose my new friends with certain ideals in mind—because they understood what was happening and how friends could move me in certain directions. Friendship was a very powerful thing in my life at that time, and I am always thankful that my parents recognized it and that God led me in the right direction.

Years later the power of friendship again affected me deeply. This time, I am happy to say, it was in a positive manner.

I was at a turning point in my life. I recognized the situation, and I knew that I had a hard decision to make. I weighed all the options before me and came to the conclusion that I needed help.

But the decision I faced was not something I could easily share with those around me. I needed an outside perspective. To whom could I turn?

One person came to my mind, an author by the name of Paul Tournier. Dr. Tournier's books had made a deep impression on me—I respected his logic, wisdom, and Christian insights. I knew little about the man except what I had read, but I had a feeling that he had all the credentials to give me the perspective I needed. I set about contacting him, a task made difficult by the fact that he did not speak English and lived in Geneva, Switzerland.

Dr. Tournier, as it turned out, was willing to set aside time to see me. Some weeks later I arrived in Switzerland as a stranger, and before much time had passed, I came to know the man as a friend.

He sliced to the heart of the matter with razor-sharp questions. Under his probing tutelage, I reexamined my problem with a new objectivity. I was confronted with things I didn't necessarily want to see. I was forced to work through questions that led to my own resolution of the problem. During my brief stay in Geneva, Dr. Tournier touched my life as few friends ever have. He helped move me, I believe, in the direction of holiness and godliness. I shall always be grateful for his positive friendship during a decision point in my life.

Friendship with God is even more powerful. And there is nothing negative about it. It always, always leads a person to peace and holiness.

The means of contacting God as we establish this relationship is prayer. We go to God because we want him to look deeply into us, to find out what needs to be removed. God is able to heal bruises, to emphasize and construct, from small seeds within each one of us, great towering oak trees. We need this kind of help. How aptly the hymn lyrics remind us, "What a Friend we have in Jesus, All our sins and griefs to bear! What a privilege to carry Everything to God in prayer!" I urge you to cultivate a friendship with God. It will make prayer so much richer as you turn to God and ask him to free his resources to work in your life.

Pray in Private

Once you acknowledge the need for a richer and deeper prayer life, how do you go about developing it? First, recognize that such a relationship with God, in prayer, develops in privacy. We find this clearly demonstrated in the way Jesus approached God in prayer. He withdrew, he left the crowd, he got away by himself. Jesus found a quiet, still place in the wilderness. Another time we read that Christ urges us to find an inner closet. Privacy is an important ingredient in prayer.

It is not easy to find a quiet place. We fill our lives with activity and with people. Perhaps we have only moments each day when we are truly alone. I urge you to find time to be alone to pray. At a Bible study, recently, a member of my congregation said, "Pastor, I have found that the only place where I can truly find quiet to pray is in my broom closet at home. I retreat there to find privacy; it is my secret place. And there I can be alone with God in prayer."

There will be times in your life when you will need to return often to your quiet place of prayer. You will go there to reinforce the spiritual strengths that come from renewing your relationship with God. Harold Medena, a prominent judge of the McCarthy era, tells an interesting story that reinforces the need for prayer in the difficult times of your life. Eleven men, charged with being communists, were tried before the Twelfth Federal District Court of New York City. Both sides in the case employed the finest trial lawyers that they could get. Unbelievable pressure came from both sides. Every legal maneuver was used to get Judge Medena to make a technical error so that a mistrial could be called. Yet he did not. In one of the most emotional moments of American history, he handed down a judgment within the law. Judge Medena was a sterling example of stability, fairness, and strength throughout the trial ordeal. What was his secret?

Two weeks later, Judge Medena spoke at the Rotary Club of Manhattan. In front of that group he shared how he had adjourned the court at odd times throughout the trial, for brief periods of time. Not until the trial ended did anyone know that during those brief recesses he had taken time to return to his private chambers to pray. Without the resources that he asked for and received from God—in the privacy of his chambers—he could not have coped with the situation before him. He told his audience that those quiet times of prayer gave him the wisdom and strength to carry on.

You must find a quiet time and a private place to pray, just as Medena did. Put your mind in neutral and shut out all the difficulties, problems, and challenges facing you. Find time to be alone with God. Teresa of Avila provides another excellent example of this principle being practiced in daily life.

Sister Teresa was well-known for her spirituality in sixteenth-century Spain. Her writings touch upon the need to be alone in prayer. She says that those who are able to shut themselves in an upper room and avoid distractions may be sure they are on the right road. This is underscored by her statement, "One cannot speak simultaneously to God and to the world." How very helpful her writing is to you and me today. Yet it was written in Spain more than four hundred years ago.

What time we give to God ought to be prime time, with concentrated effort made to shut out that which would cause us to be concerned. It takes discipline and effort, but it is a *must* as we begin to develop a good and solid prayer life. But once you are alone with God, what else must you do to make the most of your time with him?

Pray Honestly

In addition to coming to God in a quiet place, it is vitally important that you approach him with honesty. Tell him everything. Your time of prayer is not a "social gathering" where you put on a smile and tell God how wonderful everything is. In prayer time put aside the smile and unburden yourself. Be honest with the one who knows and who understands you best. To be truly honest, you must also understand and admit your feelings toward God.

How do you feel about God? Do you know that Jeremiah (in chapter 20 of the book bearing his name in the Bible) accused God of deceiving him? You have to admit, Jeremiah was being absolutely honest with God to make a statement like that in prayer. He got his feelings off his chest so that he could go on from there. Jeremiah says, "Lord, you have made me a laughingstock of all my friends. I curse the day I was born." I'd be surprised if you ever talked to God like that. I don't recall that I have ever spoken that way in prayer. If you are at all typical, you tell God how happy you are and how great everything is. You may tell a friend about your problems, but do you take those problems to God? Be honest next time you talk to God. Tell him all your fears, demolished hopes, failures, resentments, and bitterness. He is your friend. God wants to know who you hate and why. He wants to know the struggles and the frustrations. He wants you to come to him as yourself—without pretense.

In chapter 18 of Jeremiah, we find another example of coming to God in honesty. Jeremiah felt so angry with the morally corrupt young men around him that he prayed and asked that God kill them. He wanted them destroyed. "They should not even be permitted to live," Jeremiah said to God. God knew exactly what was going on in Jeremiah's life, and Jeremiah knew that God knew.

In more recent writing we find another example of the importance of honesty in prayer from a book by Henri Nouwen. Entitled *With Open Hands,* it touches on our physical approach as well as mental approach to God. He talks about how we turn to God in prayer, petition him to do things for us, tell him that we love him, and praise him—with clenched fists. Our body language betrays us, and our prayers are not really any more open than our fists. While we don't have things under control in this world, we admit it to God only reluctantly. Being honest—truly honest—forces us to be *human.* We find it very difficult to admit our human shortcomings to anyone.

Does any mother or father want to admit personal shortcomings to sons or daughters? Does any employer want to admit shortcomings to employees? Does a teacher want pupils to know that she does not know something? We are no different when we turn to God in prayer. We come to God with a facade, a separation hiding the mess and turmoil around us and inside us. We pray with clenched fists. Doing so denies God the opportunity to respond to our honesty.

Pray With Humility

Another tool a sensitive Christian uses to build a solid foundation of prayer in his life is *humility.* I believe we should match our honesty with an equal measure of humbleness. When we approach God in prayer and lay our burdens honestly before him, we must open our tightly clenched fists just as we must open our hearts and wait for God's reply.

Certain Christians have learned what humility in prayer really means. I hope that you never share their experience, but when they live through it, they tell heart-wrenching stories. For one reason or another, they have fallen into the clutches of alcoholism. Before these Christians begin the battle for recovery, they usually realize that the force eating at their insides is too strong for them to handle. They find themselves emptied of personal pride and feelings that they control their own lives. They come crashing down to the depths of despair, with a bottle in one hand and a suicide note in the other.

A woman tells the following story, which unfortunately is repeated over and over by many others.

"I pleaded with God to help me," she says softly. "But something inside me still was holding back. I couldn't let go of the bottle. 'O Lord,' I would pray, 'I'm just a hypocrite and a drunk—please help me!'

"I prayed this way for a long time. Then, at a crisis point in my life, I lost all control. It was a time shortly after I went through a divorce and I felt ostracized by my family and friends. I just didn't want to live anymore.

"I took a fifth of gin into my room, called a suicide hotline, then downed the bottle all at once. Somebody got to me after I passed out, before I died, and I wound up having my stomach pumped. Three days later I awoke in a hospital bed. As everything came back to me I crawled out of the bed somehow, got on my knees, and said, 'O God, I can't even die successfully. Just come in and do whatever you want to do with me.'

"And that was the turning point with me," the woman says. "It was total, complete submission. There was no pride left in me whatsoever. I had to hit that point before God could change me. But then he did."

I hope none of the readers of this book will need to crawl through the Slough of Despond as this woman did, but it is a spiritual truth that we attain power in our prayer life simply by recognizing that we are human and that only God is in control. True humility leads to peace, contentment, and joy.

You will find—just as I have found—that you will not always understand God's answer to your prayer. Only God sees where everything is leading. You and I are not in control, and if we ever *think* we are in control, we are sadly mistaken. Still—how often do we fret about controlling the events around us! This part of human nature is baggage we could do without as we run the race of life.

Pray knowing that God alone has the power to answer needs, lift burdens, and restore the spirit. Jesus said it this way in Mark 11:24: "You must come believing, and then all things are possible." We read in Hebrews 11:6 that: "He who believes in God, and who trusts that God is a rewarder of those who seek him" has true faith.

Pray With Faith

Faith is another important ingredient in prayer. Faith means—quite simply—being a child of God. Childlikeness is the most crucial condition for the successful practice of prayer.

How do you become a praying child of God? Start by actually deciding to do so. Faith requires that you pray believing that God will answer. No amount of honesty and humility and no private place away from the world have value if you don't pray in faith. You may not always feel like praying. Do it anyway. Do not wait until you feel like it or you are in the mood. Set up a discipline about prayer; make it a habit.

There are many things in your life that you do not feel like doing. Yet you do them anyway. If prayer seems difficult for you, you must decide that you will do it from habit. Getting into the pattern of prayer may be the most difficult obstacle for you to overcome. You will know that you have overcome it when your prayers become welcome moments in your day. Discipline yourself to get this transition started.

For many years, I held classes for community people who wanted to know the basic structure of biblical truth. One class met every Monday night in the home of a friend in a neighboring village. A member of the class, who was a salesman and extrovert but not noticeably a Christian, was Harry. His life was a mess. He was divorced, physically sick, lonesome, and in

debt. One night, as we studied the subject of faith, he propped
his foot up on a hassock. It had swelled from gout so that the
foot would not even fit into a shoe. With an exceptionally high
acid count Harry was told by his physician that he must be
hospitalized if he wanted to live. Harry chose to challenge his
doctor's judgment, delaying his admission to the hospital, to
attend our Bible study. He said he wanted to learn about God.

As I looked over at this man that particular evening, I suddenly felt a compulsion to do something that I had never done
before. I stopped the class and said, "Harry, we have been
talking about faith all evening. The blind man of Jericho believed and gained his sight from Jesus. Do you think Jesus can
heal you?" Without a moment's hesitation, Harry shot back,
"Yes, I believe that he can." I said, "I have a feeling God does
not want you sick, Harry. We are going to pray for you right
now. We're going to ask God to heal you. And each of us will
pray morning and night for healing. You pray, too, Harry, that
God will heal you."

Together we prayed. When we were finished, Harry said, "I
must confess that I really don't know how to pray. What do I
say? How do I begin?" "You are a salesman," I said. "You can
talk to people. Just talk to God as you would talk to a friend.
Be honest. Tell him what you want." "I'll do it," he replied.

Harry believed more than some of those present that evening. Going out to the car, after the Bible study ended, one of
the class members asked me, "What if Harry is not healed?" I
replied, "Did you ever ask for something from your father and
receive a no for an answer? Just trust the wisdom and the love
of God."

By Wednesday of that same week I had not heard from
Harry. So I telephoned him. He told me how he had gone
home to his apartment and flushed his pills down the drain.
This idea had *not* even come up at the Bible study and was not
and is not recommended. Then he said, "After all, if you are
going to trust God, you have to take him at his word." Then
Harry had gone to bed, tried to pray, and had finally fallen
asleep without any promise of relief from his illness. On Tues-

day morning, he awoke to a new life. His foot was completely normal. He could climb stairs again. His acid count was down.

Harry's physician was baffled. Harry believed in Christ. On Sunday morning, Harry was out in front of the church, jumping up and down and telling his story to anyone who would listen. I have rarely seen such a dramatic display of faith and thanksgiving. The prayers of faith unlocked a new life to a very new believer.

Pray for God's Guidance

You—like Harry and the others—can experience the power of prayer when you ask in faith. It does take some effort. For you to grow in your spirituality and prayer life, you must consciously practice prayer, pray honestly and humbly, pray persistently, and pray in faith. Then let God come into your life and begin to work.

I promise that if you include all these ingredients, you will be a different person. Martin Luther said it succinctly: "When I pray, I ask four questions. For what am I grateful? What do I regret? What should I ask for? What should I do?" Spend a little time being quiet, waiting for God to act, rather than talking all the time. Being open to God's guidance provides the final quality necessary to develop a healthy prayer life.

Let me illustrate. Suppose you have found your quiet place and your quiet time. You have a chair and have seated yourself comfortably in a relaxed position. Now, how do you begin to pray? *Start by claiming the presence of Christ, the living Lord.* Christ, who ascended from the grave to be with you and me and at the same time with God, is with each of us now. Ask him to come and be with you as you pray.

Pray recognizing his presence, and pray in his holy name. God is your witness. As you pray in Jesus' name, God makes your prayers authentic and real. Ask Jesus to come and stand beside you. Actually picture him there beside you as you talk with God. *Then pause to ponder your personal goals for spirituality in your life.* Be specific.

As an example of what I mean, imagine with me that your problem is controlling your emotions. Suppose you have a tendency to get excited very rapidly. You find that your temper gets away from you easily and you say things that you should not say. If this really were the case, you would wish more than anything that you could control your anger. In Proverbs 14:29 (KJV) it says, "He that is slow to wrath is of great understanding: but he that is hasty of spirit exalteth folly." We all would like to be of great understanding, not foolish. Here in the presence of Jesus Christ, we come to God in prayer with a clear objective in mind.

Next take time to praise God for the things he has done in your life. Again ponder your specific goals. Then *ask God to cleanse you and remove your sins.* Your prayer might go something like this: "O God, you are God, and there is none beside you. Let the peace of Christ flood my soul. In your presence, I put aside my burdens and fears and know that you forgive those things that I have done and should not. I open my heart to your Spirit, which dissolves every negative thought and emotion within me. I forgive everyone and pray for your forgiveness as well. I am living with expectation for the goodness that you have given me. Heal my emotions. I offer them to you here, with Christ as my witness."

Then move into the next section of your prayer. *You now become specific in asking God for direction.* Outline in detail the things you need help with. Then expect an answer or go ahead and *pledge to do what you have not been capable of doing by yourself.* This prayerful pledge is made with the expectation that God not only hears, but answers prayer. You will find that Christ will live within you and begin to work in and around you.

In a sense, you do not end your prayer, but rather leave your quiet place knowing God will be with you throughout the day. New things begin to happen. You see others as God sees them. You find that you say things that God would say to others. You find yourself reaching out to others in compassion. You find yourself going through your daily activities with a new spirit. Little by little, God will move into your life through prayer.

God also answers specific requests made by many people, every day, around the world. Sometimes he does this suddenly. In my own family, he once moved very rapidly. My little grandson was just a few months old when it became obvious that one of his legs was shorter than the other. His limbs had been twisted inside his mother's womb and had not developed correctly. His parents took him to a pediatric orthopedic surgeon in Chicago to see what could be done.

The doctor's recommendation was that he needed a series of exercises to stretch and strengthen the legs, since it appeared that the problem was in the child's hips. The surgeon cautioned that it would be a number of months before any improvement would be seen and before he could assess the need for surgery. He instructed each parent on how to do the necessary exercises and asked to see them in just three weeks to ensure that they were doing everything correctly.

The young parents decided they would pray that God would guide their hands each time they did the exercises. They prayed God would work his healing power to straighten the hips and legs. The doctor had shown them how they could tell if the exercises were having any effect upon the legs, and they watched this closely for the three weeks.

One morning, as they bathed their little son and readied themselves to travel into Chicago for the next appointment, they noticed that the legs remained unchanged. Again they prayed. I felt a strange compulsion that same morning to call them and ask them to stop on the way to the hospital. They stopped at our home, and we gathered in our kitchen for prayer. I laid my hands on the child and asked Jesus to heal him. Then I gave him back to his parents, and they left for the hospital. We were united in our belief that God could heal him, if he would.

Shortly after lunch, two very happy and thankful children stood at our door. The doctor said something had happened. My grandson's legs were perfectly normal. His hips appeared to have been restored. No cast or surgery was needed. The doctor was genuinely amazed at what he saw!

Now, two years later, there still is no sign of abnormality. Jesus heals today as he did when he lived in Galilee. God is as close to us as he was to his disciples.

Prayer Is Just the Beginning

Don't develop the qualities described in this chapter unless you expect changes in your life! Prayers that go to God persistently, as a way of life, can change your arrogance to humility, your resentment to forgiveness, your worry to patience, your fear to courage, your inferiority to a sense of worth, your vindictiveness to mercy, and strife to peace. Often these changes take place gradually. You notice them after months pass, as you take personal inventory. Sometimes the changes are swift and highly visible. Your friends may tell you something seems different about you.

As your relationship with God becomes closer, you see him moving in and around your life. You recognize events he has directed. Often his hand moves slowly, but occasionally he works like an artist in a hurry.

Prayer is just the beginning. The guidelines described in this chapter help lay a strong foundation for future spiritual growth that can expand as far and as deep as God himself. You will see your horizons expand, and you will discover a power you never dreamed of.

You also have opportunities to build on the foundation of prayer. Focusing on God and his will is an important building block—another part of the journey into joy. *Meditation* in the Christian and biblical sense is an effective way to focus on God, and we will explore that exciting concept in the next chapter.

Study Questions

1. What is the wham-zing-poof school of thought? Why doesn't it work with prayer?
2. How does a Christian develop a healthy prayer life? Name the six qualities the author has outlined for a successful one.
3. What steps can you use in praying for God's guidance? Do you use these in your own prayer life?
4. On the basis of the information in this chapter, how can you improve your own praying? Set some goals for yourself after careful thought and prayer.
5. How did you learn to pray? Did your prayer ever make a significant difference in your life or that of another person?

2

Meditation: Focusing on God

My meditation of him shall be sweet: I will be glad in the Lord.
Psalms 104:34 (KJV)

Impatience forms one of the greatest obstacles to a relationship with Christ. How often do you find yourself praying and saying, "God, I really need your help with this problem—right now." Or, "Heavenly Father, grant me the patience to be a good mother to these challenging children—today!"

We do things quickly; we want response. Scripture tells us to pray: "Speak Lord, for thy servant heareth." But so often we say: "Listen Lord, for thy servant speaketh." We ring God's doorbell and then run before he has a chance to talk to us. Our prayers turn into monologues. God scarcely has a say. In fact, many of us are skeptical that God speaks anymore.

Do you sometimes feel that whatever God had to say was all communicated when he sent Jesus Christ to live on earth? When you read John 1:14 (RSV), which says, "And the Word became flesh and dwelt among us . . . ," does it seem you are so removed from that time and place that it almost becomes unreal? Or in Hebrews you find, "God spoke with finality and completeness in his son." It seems to many Christians that God's communications with man are over. Yet we all seek closer contact with God. I believe that the secret is in prayer and quietness in God's presence—a quietness that many believers call *meditation.*

Meditation means concentrating thoughts on specific ideas, problems, and concerns—and then working through them in our minds. It differs from prayer. Prayer is talking with God. *Meditation is focusing on God and his presence.* Lazy or half-hearted Christians cannot learn this process, but those who truly seek spirituality and willingly devote time and energy to the search will succeed.

Thoughtful people sometimes ask me how meditation differs from patient, faith-filled prayer. To give an idea of the relationship and the difference, I sometimes use the analogy of seeing new vistas from a mountaintop. There is a beautiful drive that one can take in southern California, from the Pacific Ocean, near Encinitas, east through Escondido, and up to the mile-high Palomar Mountain area. In January, you can start the drive in your shirt-sleeves and finish it ninety minutes later with a toboggan ride in knee-deep snow. A first-time visitor from the Midwest is amazed by the contrast in landform and climate. What could be more stunning?

A few tourists—not many—push further east to the back side of the mountains, across an insignificant two-lane road with the name Ranchita. The road ambles east across mountain meadows and ascends a rocky ridge. Suddenly the traveler sees a sight that almost takes his breath away. He finds himself standing on the edge of cliffs that drop thousands of feet straight down to the desert floor. The afternoon sun, behind his back, flings a gigantic shadow across miles of desert, and in the distance the Salton Sea glistens in the sand. Rays of sunlight still bathe sharp desert mountains beyond the edge of the shadow, and beyond them lie other higher mountain ranges marching east toward other deserts.

The traveler realizes that the impossible has happened. His

senses, already filled with the experience of climbing from sunny beaches to snowy mountains, seem ready to burst with this new view of the California deserts.

Developing a strong prayer life, the subject of the first chapter, is a mountaintop experience. But don't stop with that. There is so much more to be learned about communicating with God!

Too many people rattle off needs, wants, burdens, joys, and praise and then stammer a quick, "Amen." That is the extent of their communication with God as their day's work begins. It misses time taken to pause, to wait, and to listen to God. Communication should be a two-way process!

Here we will explore the concept of meditation and how it helps a Christian focus on God and relate to him more deeply. We will examine how meditation can give new depth to your journey into joy. I don't know a single Christian who does not really want a richer spiritual experience and improved communication with God. Many busy Christians think they don't have the time to devote to spiritual matters, especially qualities that take time to develop. To them, I offer a challenge: "If a dear friend would show up at your door or meet you in the shopping center, would you be able to set aside fifteen minutes or a half hour to renew your friendship? If your father and mother were to ask for a few minutes of your time each day, would you tell them you are too busy? By rearranging your schedule to accommodate a friend or parent, would you throw your day into complete chaos?" By saying one is "too busy" to spend a few minutes with God, a person reveals unsettling things about his priorities and values!

Conversely, anyone who feels he has "arrived" spiritually may have missed the boat entirely. True godliness is a never-ending quest.

Several years ago a young minister apparently thought he had reached a stage of spiritual development at which God was providing him with divine personal insights. He wrote me a lengthy letter telling me that God had finally answered his prayers about his career. He was to join me as my associate pastor at this church! Now I would be the first to say that God does indeed reveal things to people, but in this case he had not revealed the same thing to me!

I had some doubts about the young minister's level of spirituality, because he apparently thought he was sending messages to God and receiving generally acceptable replies, when I knew he wasn't. In a subsequent letter, I cautioned him to be very careful concerning private information from God, especially when he began telling other people what they should or should not do. The young man may have prayed earnestly about the matter, but he had a lot to learn about other aspects of communication with God. He felt he had "arrived," but he may have been one of those who actually had missed the boat.

That young man's life may have lacked biblical, Christian meditation. Christian meditation is a means of unlocking God's resources. It helps you and me stop looking at ourselves, with all our needs and wants, and begin looking intently to God. This very personal aspect of faith can have a profound effect on our lives.

The simple shift of attention from ourselves to God is vital for spiritual growth, and naturally results from the kind of prayer life we discussed in chapter 1.

When I talk about Christian meditation, I consider that part of a human being that often is called the "inner spirit." I don't believe meditation can be successful if it is primarily an intellectual process. You must unleash your *feelings* as you meditate. A strong parallel exists between the process of Christian meditation—unlocking your inner self, your emotions, your feelings—and recent studies of the "alpha mind."

I had occasion, not long ago, to talk with the director of the Institute of the Alpha Mind in Geneva, Switzerland, about his study into the conscious and unconscious mind. He explained what the research was seeking to probe. As we talked about unlocking the real power of the human mind, he commented that we all hide remarkable power and capacities within ourselves, but they need to emerge in our lives. I could not help thinking as we talked about his studies of the subconscious that the "alpha mind" is very similar to the process of Christian meditation and focusing on God. As we focus on God we are able to unlock tremendous resources and capabilities in our lives.

I raised the question with the director of the institute that day, "Do you think that the pursuit of a deeper spiritual life through Christian meditation can be likened to the pursuit of one's own 'alpha mind'?" The idea had never occurred to him, and he had no response. As I have thought more about the comparison, I see one striking difference. We seek, as we focus our thoughts on God in meditation, to unlock all that is good and positive and righteous within us. We seek God's help as we pray and meditate. It is a good and moral process that will inevitably help us in our spiritual growth.

In contrast, the "alpha mind" research is attempting to unlock *whatever* power is there—good or evil. There is no proof that evil could not captivate an individual's mind just as easily as good, because many people are like whitewashed sepulchres. Things deep inside all of us, in fact, could produce death and destruction if allowed to take control of us. When the *Christian* dips into his "alpha mind," he focuses entirely on love, forgiveness, mercy, truth, and God's power.

In Psalms 104:34, the Psalmist says, "My meditation is sweet; I am glad in the Lord." If you look at the whole Psalm, you see the writer focusing sharply on God. The Psalmist wrote down a thoughtful account of a very personal time of reflection. How different this kind of writing is from that of authors and newspaper reporters rushing to meet deadlines as they pound out information on typewriters! The Psalmist never thought that his material would be reproduced. He simply recorded what was going on in his private life.

In Psalm 104 we read about a young shepherd boy named David. Listen to the content of his meditation as he has shared it with us, "Bless the Lord, O my soul. O Lord my God, thou art very great; thou art clothed with honour and majesty. Who coverest thyself with light as with a garment: who stretchest out the heavens like a curtain: Who layeth the beams of his chambers in the waters: who maketh the clouds his chariot: who walketh upon the wings of the wind: Who maketh his angels spirits; his ministers a flaming fire" (KJV). Then David turns to the earth and contemplates its wide and vast variety. He thinks of the night and hears the lions roaring in the dark. They roar at God to provide them with food. As the sun breaks, the lions go into their dens for rest. But man goes forth to his labors, for he labors when the sun is up.

In the agrarian culture of the Old Testament, daytime was the time for work. Filled with variety and ordered change, God's creation glorified the Creator. The Psalmist reveled in it, exclaiming, "All my meditation of him shall be sweet: I will be glad in the Lord." Look at the content of the writing in Psalm 104. It reflects emotions and feelings; David wrote it from his innermost being. Finding your inner self by focusing on God through meditation is exciting, but it is not something new to our age.

The ideas for many of these beautiful Psalms probably originated in David's mind when he was a child. Even children in those days were taught the basic concepts of meditation. As they grew up it became a natural part of their lives. Can you imagine a child meditating in our modern age? I believe that the basic skills *can* be learned by youngsters. If we shared some of the ideas contained in this chapter with our children, we could give them attitudes and skills they could draw upon later in life.

Have *you* ever practiced biblical, Christian meditation? Have you ever thought about it? Have you ever really tried to do it? I hope the advice in this chapter will give you an understanding of how meditation fits into the total picture as a part of your spiritual walk. I also hope you will begin a regular program of meditation yourself!

Christian Meditation Is Not Transcendental

I think we should be clear on the difference between Christian meditation and the popular "transcendental meditation," or TM. TM is the act of clearing the mind of all distractions. As he concentrates on a tone, a vowel, or a syllable, the practitioner of TM tries to make his mind a clean slate. The purpose is to step back from the activity and business of life and to have a period of time each day when the mind remains at peace. Successful TM entails the achievement of that emptying process each time one meditates. Christian meditation brings an added dimension that sets it apart from TM. Our purpose in spending time quietly is to ready ourselves for God's message. He may answer a particular prayer, quiet a troubled heart, provide strength, or give guidance. Our purpose is not achieving emptiness, but finding a filling of God's Spirit within.

We already discussed the common use of meditation in Old Testament times. The Bible also tells us that it was practiced in New Testament times. Jesus rose long before dawn to be off by himself, away from his disciples, to pray and meditate. We read of his practice in Mark 1:35. Right up to the modern age meditation has been part of the lives of godly men and women. History provides many examples of individuals who understood that same need to be alone, apart from the world, to be ready to hear God through meditation. Many names are familiar to you: Saint Augustine, Saint Francis of Assisi, Bernard of Clairvaux, Brother Lawrence, Saint Teresa of Avila, and Saint John of the Cross. Among our contemporaries we find individuals like Frank Laubach and Evelyn Underhill. The tradition of the church has long included meditation.

Reading biographies or studying Scripture, we find many examples of people who have really grasped the power of faith by taking time for solitude and meditation. I have had many opportunities to speak with individuals who believe in Christian principles, intellectually, but find the power of faith itself elusive. You may have had the same feeling at some point in your life. I know I have felt that what I understood about my Christian belief was somehow not crossing over into my walk in faith. Meditation and prayer provide the bridge between our intellectual acceptance of God's truth and our spiritual embrace of that truth personally.

Certainly if we can gain any lesson from the practice of TM by so many in recent years, it is that they made it a discipline. I think you will find that putting forth that same level of self-discipline into biblical, Christian meditation will bring forth exciting results. Before we look at the *how* of meditation, let's be sure we are in accord in our basic definition of *meditation*.

What Is Meditation?

What is Christian meditation, and how does it differ from devotions, prayer, or the study of Scripture? I would define devotions as a process that joins together Bible study and prayer. In a real sense the two together become the preamble to your time of meditation. Prayer itself is a more formal time of communication with God that includes the ingredients of praise and adoration. Devotions can be alone or as a part of a group, but always include prayer. Meditation demands that we are absolutely alone. It requires concentrating—and *concentrating* is a stronger word than *thinking* or *pondering*—on an idea, a truth, or a person, with the intent of comprehension and understanding.

In meditation, the mind runs free, yet focuses on the concept or idea chosen. Intense thought takes determination and discipline. It is not easy. But how many worthwhile things in your life are easily gained? In my own life, the most worthwhile achievements have taken the greatest effort, concentration, and hard work on my part. I also need to make sacrifices of time and energy to obtain them!

Learning to Meditate

I'll begin this section by assuming that, for you, meditation is a lost art. At best, it probably is an elusive idea you have never been able to study. That's understandable. In our culture we're constantly being driven to perform, earn, produce, and succeed—not relax and reflect. It would probably be easier for us to understand meditation if we had at least seen our parents practicing it, but I believe the skills were lost to the preceding generation, too.

So we will start fresh. As with anything unfamiliar, we must begin with a commitment to learn. We need to practice and repeat certain procedures, perhaps at first failing and then gaining in proficiency. Slowly we comprehend what it is all about.

Interestingly, Scripture offers no definition of meditation. People are often described as meditating, but meditation itself is not defined. People simply did it. It was an accepted practice as natural to them as balancing a checkbook is to us. What did they *do?* David probably meditated alone in the hills. In Genesis 24:63 we read that Isaac left his home in the evening to go out into the fields to meditate. The workers were gone by that time, and Isaac had no distractions as he spent time with God.

Be Relaxed and Quiet

To meditate, find the kind of place that David or Isaac found. You need to be undisturbed. Since many of us can't wander off into the hills or fields, we need to adjust our urban environment. Pull the plug on the telephone. Turn off the television or radio. Find a familiar place that will not distract your thoughts. Make yourself comfortable. In my readings, I find that people who meditate will stand, sit, or even recline. Being comfortable is important. Do what works for you—don't worry too much about what other people may recommend.

Some of the older church-related colleges (and even some new ones) provide "quiet rooms" where students can be alone with their thoughts. I sometimes wonder how many students actually use them for the intended purposes, but their existence may be reminiscent of times past when students actually did meditate. In rural areas of the Midwest, one occasionally finds a wayside chapel. Again, something about such a place invites reflection and possibly even meditation.

One of my colleagues, a well-known writer and lecturer, meditates while standing at an elevated desk. Another friend has built a special room in his garden where he screens out noise and feels close to nature. Many people come to the garden chapel of the church where I am pastor, to enjoy the presence of trees and plants and the lilt of running water over a rocky fountain waterfall. I have preached some sermons on this subject over the months, and I believe some of our people practice meditation as they sit in the chapel.

Relax, but stay alert. You need to keep your mind sharp and active.

Choose a Topic

Once you are comfortable, choose your subject. Do you need to concentrate on your relationship with another person? Do you need to meditate about a difficult situation within your home or at work? Do you need patience or forgiveness?

Let yourself become mentally involved in this relationship, difficult situation, or concept. Think of a keynote word and repeat it over and over to yourself. (Those of you familiar with TM might wonder if I'm simply borrowing a method from TM. Emphatically, no! In TM, a practitioner uses a particular word as a *mantra* and repeats it over and over in a ritualistic way. What I'm describing in biblical, Christian meditation is a mental exploration of a single concept. The idea is to focus the mind on the concept, not just achieve a relaxed "alpha mind" state. I'll discuss this further a little later in this chapter.)

As an example of Christian meditation, let's assume that you have chosen to consider the idea of *love*. Begin to think about love. Repeat the word to yourself. Let your mind take the idea and run with it. You may choose a scene from the Bible from which you would like to gain new insight. Concentrate on this scene and let your mind explore all its implications. Perhaps you have chosen to visualize Jesus by the open tomb at Bethany when he called to Lazarus. See him standing there. Imagine the crowd that gathered around him as he called to Lazarus. Take yourself there as you meditate. Experience the intensity of feeling in the air as people watched to see what he would do. Feel the bitterness of those who were criticizing him in jealousy. Let your mind wander over that experience just as the Psalmist let his mind wander over his subject. Be open to whatever will come into your mind as you meditate.

One of the most moving experiences of my life was in the early morning hours on Mount Sinai. I sat alone on a huge rock, visualizing the return of Moses. As I meditated I could see the crowded valley filled with eager faces, uplifted and silent as their leader read the Ten Commandments for the first time. While dawn broke across the sky that morning, my soul became revived in a very mystical way. I must confess that although I tried to explain that experience later, in one of my sermons, I failed even to scratch the surface of that deep and profound time of meditation.

Be Patient as You Meditate

The secret of meditation is not to be anxious about the results. In fact, you may choose to begin with just five minutes at a time. Nothing may happen the first time you meditate. Even on the second or third time, you may find that you are not gaining any particular insight. Be quiet and keep your mind focused on your selected subject. If you try to force a structure on your meditation, you will fall into the trap of listening to yourself instead of God.

If you really believe that the Spirit of God is within you, be very quiet. Then God will speak. Paul points out in his writings that the indwelling of the Holy Spirit reveals the deep things of God. He says, "The rulers of this age will never comprehend the wisdom of God which God has revealed to us through the Spirit. For the Spirit searches everything, even the depths of God." In 1 Corinthians 2:9, 10 we find Paul telling us that we will hear things we never thought possible—things from God, both constructive and positive.

I remember one occasion when I had chosen *joy* as my focal point for meditation. I explored the idea that the joy I was seeking was not really for myself, but resulted from centering my focus on God. I began to picture truly joyous people. I thought of particularly joyful times in my own life. I saw joy in children; I saw joy in families. As I visualized joy, I found my thoughts moving to the idea of joy for my enemies. My meditation helped me to see that God's love could and would manifest itself in me—even to my enemies. I came away from that meditation time better prepared to reach out in love to those around me because I had visualized myself doing so with God's divine help.

Jesus taught us to pray and meditate. He also instructed us on the meaning of forgiveness when he said, "For if you forgive men their trespasses, your heavenly Father also will forgive you" (Matthew 6:14 RSV). On another occasion he taught us, in John 15:12 (KJV), that we should, ". . . love one another, as I have loved you." And he promised that we will come to a clear understanding of his teachings if we rely on the inner leading of the Holy Spirit when he said, "The . . . Holy Spirit . . . will teach you all things, and bring to your remembrance all that I have said to you" (John 14:26). Having these passages from Scripture in mind as I meditated on love made the meditation time that much richer for me. You may also find a reference from Scripture helpful because it can help you to focus your thoughts as you begin to meditate.

As I mentioned earlier, focusing on a passage of Scripture or even a biblical story is quite a bit different from the approach that you find in transcendental meditation. Let me explain the difference. Eastern mysticism compels individuals to sit and contemplate with the aid of some meaningless syllable, called a mantra. They simply repeat it over and over during meditation. It is relaxing. The brain's subconscious or alpha state is enhanced as the blood pressure drops. For all practical purposes, you are at rest—nearly sleeping—yet conscious enough to repeat your mantra. Physically, transcendental meditation works fine. But, as Martin Gruber says in his book, *Between Man and Man,* writing as a past devotee of transcendental meditation, he realized that he only talked to himself. In reality he had no relationship to anything or anyone else. That kind of meditation is without content, nothing more than humanism in its purest form. How fortunate we are to have such depth and understanding possible through the Christian meditation experience!

Christian meditation centers on God. We do not simply open ourselves and our minds to whatever would fill them—or empty them for that matter. By contrast to all other forms of meditation, Christian meditation empties our minds and spirits in order to fill them with what God has for us. That is what we are listening for. Meditation extends prayer to a much deeper level as we ask God to reveal to us what it means to be joyous, loving, or to experience one of the other fruits of the Spirit or Christian virtues. God speaks to us in our meditation; we listen.

The self-denial in Eastern meditation is not found in Christian meditation. You do not empty yourself to become *nothing*. You seek to empty yourself to become *something*. Your meditation will enhance what and who you are, for the express purpose that God intends. Meditation is really the process of becoming vulnerable to God's leading.

Be Open as You Meditate

Is something on your mind today? Does something trouble you? Are you faced with a decision that you really feel you need to examine thoroughly? Who are you? What is your weakness? Be open to your needs and meditate on a positive scriptural answer. I think Christians tend to try to meditate on lofty topics and scenes from Scripture while their hearts remain heavy with a personal problem. Turn your meditation loose on that concern. Let God speak to you about it. Pray about it, put in the details, and turn it over to Jesus—then meditate. Let God give you the insight you need, the wisdom, the understanding, the right words and direction. Focus on God and unlock his power in your life. Be open as you meditate.

For example, imagine you react too quickly with bitterness and hatred. You wish you had more compassion and love. Then meditate on the concepts of gentleness and forgiveness.

Find a passage from Scripture, such as 2 Corinthians 10:1, which talks about "the gentleness of Christ" or Galatians 5:22, 23, which explores gentleness as a fruit of the Spirit. Or meditate on the story of the paralytic (Mark 2:5 RSV) to whom Jesus said, "My son, your sins are forgiven." Picture in your mind the joy of the forgiven and the peace that calms the heart Jesus touches. Become like the poet who exclaimed, "May my meditation be pleasing to him, as I rejoice in the Lord. . . . Praise the Lord, O my soul . . ." (Psalms 104:34, 35 NIV).

Leave your mind open and ask God to give you ideas, revelations, and feelings about gentleness and forgiveness in your life. Let whatever comes to mind sink into your subconscious, penetrating into the depths of your being. Let it establish its imprint so indelibly upon you that, when you meet situations that day or a week after you have meditated several times on the subject, you will not react as you did in the past.

As you consider these concepts, you will discover what it means to be as gentle and forgiving as Jesus. Strive to be like him. That is the reason to make the time in your busy day to meditate. This spiritual discipline will move you toward a more Christ-like life, if you let it. It must be important to you. Frankly, if you don't feel as if meditation is important right now, don't do it. Perhaps someday soon it will be important enough for you to begin—and then it will work for you.

Be Transformed Through God's Power

What a tremendous transformation will take place inside you when you meditate. I know it will. Such change as the result of meditation has been part of my experience. A group of men in my church and I differed in our view of a particular subject and had not been able to communicate our differing beliefs to each other, much less reach understanding or accord. The issue itself is no longer important. But the experience of praying about it and then meditating on it made a tremendous impact on its resolution. Did I meditate about the men themselves or even the issue? No. I found I needed to meditate on a larger picture.

I chose to envision seeing these individuals—my greatest antagonists within that church—in the presence of God. I contemplated God's love for these people and for me. I pictured Jesus within me, reaching out to them in love. My meditation was entirely focused on positive thoughts about our contact with each other and the need to react in love. I should add that the men with whom I had this difference of opinion knew nothing of my meditation. Yet, I felt the need to spend a considerable amount of time on this matter. What resulted? Was everything quickly and easily corrected? No. But I found within myself the ability to react to these fellows in a loving and understanding manner that got us through the strife and finally enabled us to reach an effective resolution of the situation. I was open to God as I meditated and he gave me the insight that was needed. But, you know, meditation did not change my personality, which remained just as it had been. If anything changed, it was my character. Character comes from the depth of our being. You cannot maneuver or engineer that kind of change yourself. Only God can provide the growth of character needed to overcome the problem at hand. Meditation—focusing on God and being open to his message—is the secret. Wait for God to speak, listen quietly.

Remember Psalms 91:1, which says, "He who dwells in the secret place of the most high shall abide under the shadow of the almighty." There you will find God. Discover that quiet center where you can seek God and he, in turn, can *find* you. Out of that experience, your conscience will be so sharpened that you will not want to offend God. Your heart becomes so affected that you keep all your love for him. Your mind perceives his will and his word in the critical times when life would defeat you.

Your actions betray your selflessness for others' well-being. You begin to stand fast in the stormiest gale, with new independence and strength. With God's guidance, you determine where things are going, instead of giving in to the pressures of society.

Through meditation you will find the power to defeat weaknesses in your character, which you have been willing to accept in the past. Paul's words come alive: ". . . It is no longer I who live, but Christ who lives in me . . ." (Galatians 2:20 RSV). "I can do all things in him who strengthens me" (Philippians 4:13 RSV).

Study Questions

1. What is meditation? How does it differ from prayer? Why is it important in the Christian's life?
2. Describe the differences between Christian meditation and transcendental meditation. What are the benefits of Christian meditation?
3. Have you ever tried to practice Christian meditation? What happened? Can you set goals for yourself in this area?
4. What place would you choose to meditate? Are you aware that members of your family meditate? Do they have a place of peace and quiet?

3

Solitude: Removing the Distractions

Be still, and know that I am God. . . .
Psalms 46:10 (KJV)

We have explored the role of prayer in your spiritual life. Then we looked at how meditation can enhance your prayers by teaching you to concentrate on a specific thought or idea and clear your mind so God can speak to you. *Solitude* is the next important step on the spiritual journey toward a richer relationship with God.

I'm sure you have a busy life. In fact, the typical Christian probably will respond that it is *more than busy*—it is downright hectic! I knew a young family once, in which both the husband and wife pursued demanding professional careers. They had two children, and to give the children proper care they utilized day-care centers, baby-sitters, occasional help from relatives, and favors from neighbors. Their daily schedules weren't just lists of times and engagements, but complex flow charts mapping out when and where they would be during the day, who would be making the trip from the day-care center to the baby-sitter, who would contact Thursday's sitter, and how the children would be transported from home to a relative on a school vacation day. If a child became sick, they panicked, because neither parent could afford to interrupt a busy professional schedule for a day or two. They spent their days rushing from one project to another, and I'm sure the days turned into a blur of passing weeks. They never had time to pause for reflecting on anything, and I'm sure if I had begun discussing solitude with them, they would have told me to go back to the ivory tower and leave them to their pursuits.

You may not be locked into an extreme situation like that, but you might catch glimpses of your own life in that story. Solitude might seem like an impossible dream, but it also might benefit you in your harried existence! Let's look at this method of removing distractions and drawing closer to God— something more important than a career or keeping sixteen appointments in a day.

Recently, in Wales, I attended a study session at a residential library. While there I had an experience that gave me insight into the concept of solitude and its role in a person's spiritual life. Wales is rich in scenery, as any tourist knows. The countryside seems to beckon one into its valleys, glades, and winding paths.

While studying there, I met Father Mark Gibbard, an Anglican monk and member of the order of Saint John the Evangelist. I was studying in Saint Deiniol's Library in Hawarden, Wales, where Father Mark lives and writes.

Mark Gibbard is one of those remarkable elderly saints who has spent many years traveling, lecturing, praying, and publishing. He enjoys exceptional health due to his attitude, regular periods of exercise, and a careful diet. His sparkling, penetrating eyes welcomed me as a friend. He was—I sensed the moment I met him—a remarkable man.

Late each afternoon, Father Mark takes a walk through the nearby fields and gardens of Gladstone Castle. I had the opportunity to join him for one of those afternoon walks. "This is my time of meditation and quiet," he explained to me. I must confess that I had looked forward to joining him on his daily walk with unashamed awe, for he truly was a deeply mystical person. What would it be like to be out in the fields with such an expert in prayer and solitude? Would God be closer through some special revelational act or sound as I joined Father Mark for the afternoon?

Our walk began with some polite and meaningless talk. I was anxious to ask him questions that were of particular interest to me, questions regarding spiritual disciplines. I wanted to know how he practiced them and how I could improve.

As we walked, it did not take long before it became strangely quiet. At first I thought I should say something. But I decided it would be an intrusion into his thoughts. After walking on for a few moments in silence, Father Mark stopped, looked at me, and said, "How good to be in the presence of the Creator. How wonderful that he who made all things also made you and me to fill a very unique place in his plans. We must try above all else to accept ourselves and to listen quietly for his leading."

It was a moment I will never forget. The breeze drifted through the fragrant meadows and snatched at the collar of my shirt. The warm sunlight painted shadows across Father Mark's expressive face. The great, blue sky stretched from hilltop to hilltop. And in the midst of this beautiful world, God had made me, one of a kind, different from all others, for some special spot in his vast, eternal kingdom!

Suddenly, as if space and time had lost meaning, an hour and a half had passed, and we were back at the gate where we had started. It occurred to me that we had finished our walk in silence—several minutes of silence. We had gone beyond the need to talk. Friends do not need to talk to prove their interest in each other. I felt Father Mark and I had become friends.

I should caution that I do not extol less talking between friends. Talk can be necessary and good. But if you need silence, saying nothing can be an equally acceptable part of friendship. Stillness in the presence of a friend can be a precious experience. It reinforces mutual support and trust.

I have many friends, but few with whom I can share moments of silence. Usually we talk. Silence is embarrassing. We are friends because of mutual interests, community interest, or Christian activities. When we get together, we feel we must be saying and doing things. Silence becomes a waste of time. When we have covered the subject matter, we adjourn and move on. These friends tell me that such activism makes the world go around—and around and around, and around.

To borrow from an adage, these friends and I produce plenty of smoke, but not much fire.

If we had been with Elijah in the cave, waiting for God to speak, we probably would have rushed into the earthquake and tossed around a few rocks ourselves. We would have huffed and puffed right along with the windstorm God sent. We would have been so busy talking about things that we probably wouldn't even have heard the still, small voice when he did speak!

God wants us to consciously come into his presence and be still. He wants us to wait for him to speak and to lead. He wants us to place our minds in "neutral" while mystically remaining aware of his presence through Christ. This is called solitude. It is something many people experience but few learn to appreciate.

Scripture tells us, "Draw near unto God and he will draw near unto you" (James 4:8). Jesus said, "Come unto me, all ye that labour and are heavy laden, and I will give you rest" (Matthew 11:28 KJV). My friend, Father Mark, was content to allow me to be silent while we walked together. I found in that experience a lesson in solitude. God speaks in new and inspiring ways as we wait for him in silence. Special friends are individuals whom you trust, persons of integrity on whom you can call—anytime—day or night. Friends are always ready to respond. Whether you succeed or fail, whether you have good things to say or bad things, your friends will want to listen to you.

A friend is the kind of person with whom you want to associate. Even if you go with that good friend to a gathering of friends, the most precious moment comes when you and that friend are alone. When just the two of you share time, you can really bare your soul and find the intimacy of understanding.

Friendship as we know it in our daily lives is only a glimmer of the deep relationship that we can enjoy with God. Solitude—the conscious act of removing the distractions around us—is the key to our relationship with God. Let's explore, together, a bit more about friendship. Suppose you have a good friend who also heads your local school, or manages the place where you work, or who is a leader in government. You and your good friend talk often. Your friend advises you and lets you in on secrets of what goes on behind the scenes. You are "in the know"; you have an inside track. When someone else approaches you with petty gossip or rumors, you disregard them because you know better. Things are not what rumor reports. You experience confidence and a sense of stability in the midst of conjecture and false assumptions.

But you recognize that no matter how much "sway" a friend can exercise in your life, he or she is not really in control. I recall an excellent example of this. A reporter remarked to me some time ago that Leonid Brezhnev—the late premier of the Union of Soviet Socialist Republics—said, "If God is willing, we will find a solution for peace in the world."

The reporter felt a bit amused to think that Brezhnev—the leader of an atheistic nation—would say such a thing. Brezhnev apparently recognized that every human being knows life is beyond his power to control. Ultimately we all recognize that the control comes from somewhere else. And we know that human beings are only mortal. Your best friend may not stay around tomorrow. He may move away or even die. There are no guarantees.

Wouldn't it feel tremendously strengthening to have a friend who is divine? Can you imagine a friend unlimited by the things that limit us? God is that friend!

By now, you have raised the question, "Isn't solitude a condition in which you are alone?" Or, "What does friendship have to do with solitude in my life?" How do you practice solitude in the presence of anyone else—even your best friend?

Your questions are entirely appropriate. Human solitude requires that you be alone, away from all your friends. We often
mistake solitude for loneliness, because it is viewed simply as
being apart from friends. I want you to consider now the solitude achieved through closeness to God. In the spiritual sense
that we are seeking to understand it, this demands a relationship with God. It is really the act of being "with God," just as
you would spend time with a very dear friend. That is why we
have explored the qualities of friendship. You and I easily understand the friends around us each day; now let's approach
God as the same kind of friend. Learn to approach solitude in
this way, and you will find it much easier to grasp.

In solitude, we learn how to draw closer to God. We quietly
open our lives to him. We are not concerned mainly with
prayer (talking to God) or meditation (focusing on God), but
just on letting God fill our lives as we remain open to his presence.

In Psalms 46:10, the writer tells us that we must learn to be
quiet and know God. The Psalmist reflects on the history of Israel—the history of God's people. He talks of the God of Jacob
being his refuge. Who is the "God of Jacob"? He is the same
God who appeared to Jacob when Jacob ran from his brother,
Esau. The story is recorded in Genesis 28.

Fearful for his life, Jacob headed for his uncle Laban's
place. He traveled light and avoided main roads. After the first
day's journey, in a solitary field, Jacob rested his head on a
stone and went to sleep. There, alone in the field at night, he
had a vision of a ladder stretching to heaven. At the top of the
ladder was God, reassuring him and promising that he would
be with Jacob if Jacob would trust him. Jacob found that reas-
surance in solitude. He was removed from the distractions of
life—alone with no one but God.

Many years later, as recorded in Genesis 32, Jacob came
back to his homeland to reconstruct his own relationship with
his brother Esau. Expecting a bitter, perhaps bloody confron-
tation, Jacob spent the night before meeting Esau on the banks

of the brook Jabbok. He was completely alone. The Bible tells us that in his solitude he turned to God.

From out of the darkness came a stranger. He crashed into Jacob and with strong arms locked him in a wrestler's grip. Jacob recovered his balance and began wrestling with all his might. The contest lasted all night. Jacob refused to give up, and the stranger allowed him to continue. What was going on in Jacob's mind? How could he fight furiously all night?

I think Jacob realized that the stranger in the darkness was God himself. Jacob had spent time with God many times, and God had appeared to him before, in solitude. He must have sensed that God was again appearing to him. As Jacob reflected on this wrestling match, he recognized that God had used it to teach a very important lesson. No person could shake Jacob to the core again—not even Esau, with a force of 400 mounted men. In solitude, Jacob had found the strength to face his brother.

Down through the years, when men and women have found God, they have experienced a desire to spend time with him. A yearning comes with tasting the life we can know in God's presence. So new believers seek to know God in a personal way. Jesus demonstrated this same desire to spend time alone with his Father. He knew God in a deep and personal way. We read in Mark 1 that at his busiest times, Jesus would go out, alone, to spend time with God in solitude. In the Garden of Gethsemane, facing death on a cross, he spent time with God.

In Matthew 6:6, Jesus urges us to go into our inner closets. We must seek a quiet place where we can be all alone. Spend time with God in solitude. God makes it clear that this will reveal inner strength that never before seemed possible. But it takes solitude to unlock that inner power. In a sense, prayer, meditation, and solitude are all variations of the basic need in each of us to take time to be with God. We need to make it a part of each day. Spending time talking to God, pondering his direction for us, and just being alone with him are three vital secrets to spiritual growth. But are these secrets really something new?

Reading in the Old and New Testaments, and throughout history, we find that the saints spent time alone. The saints knew and understood how to draw on their inner resources through solitude. John was alone on the Lord's day when he penned the last book of the Bible, the book of Revelation. God was there with him. The Psalmist writes, "Be still, and know that I am God . . ." (Psalms 46:10 KJV). God was there with the Psalmist, and God remains here with you, moving in your life, to accomplish his ends. Find time to be alone with him. Learn to draw on his power within you.

Throughout history there has been a mysterious undercurrent of spirituality directed from above. The way in which you and I can tap into that power is through a relationship with God himself. He waits for us. He is waiting for you. The people of the Old Testament experienced a relationship with God. In the New Testament, Paul reflects that God is able to supply all our needs. But you and I must spend time alone with him, time of quiet and solitude. "Be still, and know that I am God. . . ."

In the past few years, I have discovered that solitude is most effective when I literally close the door on my busy life to spend time alone with God. In the development of any deep relationship, one must spend time alone with another person. Our relationship with God is no exception. It takes commitment on my own part. When I want to spend time alone with God—away from the world—this is what I do.

Finding Time Alone With God—How to Begin

I begin by finding a comfortable position in a favorite place. I close my eyes, physically, to help me shut out the world mentally. My imagination usually takes me to a tranquil spot—a familiar place along the lake or by an ocean shore or in a field or garden. Even a picture of such a place changes the scenery of the mind.

Once I have found that comfortable position and set the scene, I begin with prayer. I often say something like, "Dear Father, I am happy to be with you for a few moments. . . ."

Then I say, "Thank you for making such a beautiful place for your pleasure and mine." I follow this with a time of waiting and listening. It is, quite simply, a time of being alone with God.

Unlike prayer and meditation, solitude is a time of stillness, waiting, listening. We can easily understand that prayer does not always include solitude. One can pray while sitting shoulder to shoulder with 200 other people on a commuter train. A mother can pray while holding a crying baby. Soldiers pray in the heat of battle. Meditation is adjusting the lenses of the mind so God is in sharp focus. This activity may take place in a quiet room or a darkened chapel. The mind remains alert and active. As we meditate, God enlightens us about a particular truth or a person. Meditation could be called a conscious effort to fill the mind with certain kinds of thoughts.

Solitude requires the emptying of the mind. While a quiet place is one prerequisite of meditation, it stands at the core of solitude. Solitude is an escape from all the busyness and pressure of life to be in the presence of God. We do not attain the blessings of solitude through conscious effort or by drawing upon spiritual skills. The blessings come from a deep and meaningful *relationship*—a little like the relationships we have in marriage or family life.

Good relationships take years to develop. They take commitment, communication, and sometimes sacrifice. So, too, the blessings of solitude grow richer over the years. These blessings come more and more easily as a bond is strengthened.

The way our family celebrates Christmas offers an analogy of the way prayer, meditation, and solitude interrelate. We enjoy coming together as a family every Christmas—parents, children, and grandchildren. Some weeks before the event, we talk about when the reunion will take place, who will come, and what kind of presents the grandchildren would appreciate. Certain needs are expressed, and many details are considered. We talk. In a way, that reflects the communication we have with God through prayer. A grandchild might send us a list of fourteen things he or she wants, and we are glad to receive it.

Then comes a time of reflecting on the other members of the family. We consider presents, but also travel plans, lodging, and an itinerary while they are back at home. We focus our thoughts on others. In a small way, that could be compared to meditating. We think about certain things, certain people, and ways to make Christmas an enjoyable experience for them.

Finally Christmas comes. We gather in the living room, sing a few songs, watch the children open the presents, and enjoy one another's company. Conversation tends to be at a minimum. I can feel perfectly comfortable sitting back in my chair and just letting the laughter and sights of loving faces flow over me. I don't have an agenda, a sermon, deadlines, or pressures. I just enjoy the presence of the people who mean the most to me. Again the experience is just a bit like enjoying the relationship with God that has built up over many years.

The three steps toward spirituality that we have considered in the first three chapters of this book are interrelated. One leads to the other, and when all three are exercised in harmony, rich blessings result.

Through solitude we discover God. He becomes real to us— as real as the faces of loved ones. God lives inside of us.

My friend, I hope and pray that you can feel close to God in your own life.

The chief executive officer of a major corporation told me he closes his door every day for ten or fifteen minutes and tells his secretary he does not want to be disturbed. He wants quiet time, time to be alone with God. In the midst of a Michigan Avenue corporate headquarters of an international business, there is peace and quiet for a few moments in that leader's office. That is his source of strength!

If you find it difficult to put things out of your mind, let me suggest something. People through the ages have used the Jesus prayer, "Lord be merciful to me, a sinner." Perhaps you want the abbreviated version, "Lord have mercy." Focus your mind on the words. In two or three minutes you will discover that the distractions have disappeared. You will find a willingness to be receptive to whatever God wants to say to you. You will begin to sense his presence.

Perhaps you will need one day (or two or three) a year just to go away and be by yourself. You may need to take time to learn, to consider those things that come in the quiet place. But it takes patience, nonprogrammed waiting. It demands a strong desire to be with the one who said, "I do not call you servants . . . I call you my friends" (John 15:15). God wants to be with you. "Be still, and know that I am God."

Seeking Close Relationships: A Human Trait

Something inside each of us demands intimacy and commitment. It is part of our fabric as human beings. People who have not found a quiet center of strength in their lives through a relationship with God strive to find it in many places. They scurry about frantically, attending meetings, parties, and social events.

Recently I attended a party staged to welcome some people to an organization to which I belong. I admit my heart was not in the gathering. I had several other things to do, and I was there out of a sense of duty rather than love for the organization. I found myself watching the people around me playing relationship games. Meaningless pleasantries were on everyone's lips, superficial conversations replaced real communication, and people on the fringes of the group looked extremely uncomfortable. But the party went on, the conversation flowed, and people drifted from one social group to the next as if they were having a grand time.

It struck me, then, that it was all a very human effort to build relationships—any kind of relationship. Not only do we fear loneliness, but we go through all kinds of ritualized efforts to come into contact with someone else.

Some people get up in the morning and, in order not to miss anything, turn on the radio or television. They reach out through the broadcasting media to contact another human. They want to hear the familiar voice of the anchorperson on the "Today" show. A little later in the day a homemaker might tune in the struggles of the friends she has come to know through soap operas. Loneliness—lack of relationships—is a

fearful thing, and if we can't fill our lives with true relationships, we at least fill them with talking voices, music, and noise.

Some people seek to fill the void of shallow or nonexistent
relationships by becoming "joiners." They organize groups.
They come together for a variety of purposes, all masking the
real need to overcome their fear of being alone. They come to
receive, not to give. A few months ago, while on a trip to North
Carolina, I became a part of another structured "community."
The setting was the cabin of a jet. It became an artificial community as passengers joked, laughed, and ate together. This
feeling of community was successfully orchestrated by the
stewardesses. But the moment the plane touched down and arrived at the gate, that sense ended. I pitied a dear little elderly
woman caught in the massive, crushing rush for the door of the
plane. Treated with kindness and gentleness, she chatted with
those around her while we were in the air; now that we were
back to the reality of the airport and rushing to find luggage,
taxis, and friends, she was pushed aside without concern by
those around her. No continuing friendships and no real commitments developed on the plane. There was plenty of smoke,
but no real fire.

The attempts at building relationships on airplanes illustrate
the powerful need for intimate relationships. Another evidence
of the unending quest for nearness and relief from loneliness is
the peddling of cheap sex. How common it has become! Radio
and television programs are laced with double meanings and
innuendo. At its extreme, this becomes pornography. Our society suffers with the mistaken belief that if individuals can get
close physically, that will satisfy them. How fleeting the experience is. I have had men come to me and break down and weep
in my office because they have gotten involved in a cheap
physical relationship with a woman. They end up no more sat-
isfied than when they began. Lives are threatened, marriages
sometimes shattered. And they continue to suffer from loneliness, perpetuated by people who come together to *get* but
never to *give*.

So very unlike the situations and people I have just described, there are those individuals who practice solitude. They have found, in their quiet place, the presence of the Creator. They have discovered, in that special spot, that God himself loves his people just as they are. That is why he made them. It is the way he made you. You are like no one else—with no apologies. Your relationship with God should be just as unique as you yourself are.

The deepest relationship is forged in solitude. That relationship is between you and God, through Christ, his Son. He is your greatest friend today, tomorrow, and in eternity. When you spend time with him, something happens inside you. The events that transpire—politically, economically, and socially—in your community and around the world, take on a different tone. There is a larger context in which you begin to live. You are able to form community because you have something to give to others. You are strong within yourself and confident because of the association you have with God. You can allow others their privacy as you share with them your friend: God.

As we move ahead to the next chapter, we enter a new section of this book: "Journey Into Personal Growth." In it we will consider ways that God has provided to simplify your life, build self-esteem, and discipline your body.

Study Questions

1. Define *solitude*. How does it differ from *loneliness?*
2. The author draws a correlation between *solitude* and *friendship*. Can this work in your friendships with other people? If so, how?
3. How is friendship with God different from friendship with others? Is solitude necessary to develop this relationship? Why or why not?
4. How are prayer, meditation, and solitude interrelated? Why is each important? What benefits do they produce in the Christian's life?
5. Does the "American way of life" eliminate the possibility of solitude? How can the cycle be broken?

Part II

Journey Into Personal Growth

4

Self-esteem: Accepting His Creation

We love him, because he first loved us.
1 John 4:19 (KJV)

Two farm boys and their city slicker cousin inched cautiously across the barnyard. The huge holstein bull eyed them across twenty feet of hard-packed dirt. He was the biggest animal on the farm—more than a ton of quivering bone and muscle.

The boys walked sideways, eyes locked on the bull. They knew that if they broke the gaze and bolted for the fence, he would be after them like a locomotive. The animal danced a little on his front feet, snorted softly, and lowered his head.

The younger farm boy and his cousin looked yearningly at the fence by the barn. The ten yards between them and the fence could have been ten miles. The boys, six and seven years old, respectively, had no illusions of winning a race with an animal as powerful as the holstein. Their heads barely came up to his shoulder. All three children together hardly weighed one-tenth as much as the monster of the barnyard.

"He's going to charge," the six-year-old whispered to his brother.

The bull lowered his head still farther. He snorted again and shook his massive neck.

"If he comes after us, you two head for the fence as fast as you can," the older boy said quietly out of the corner of his mouth.

"So b-b-big!" the cousin stammered, his eyes the size of the reflectors lining the driveway.

The bull might have heard the comment or seen a movement he didn't like. Or maybe he was trying to protect his territory. But for whatever reason, he gave another snort and lunged forward. That couldn't really be called a full-scale charge, but it sent the younger boys racing for the fence as fast as their legs would pump. The bull must have enjoyed a little surge of self-importance, because he increased his speed and let out another snort, loud enough to be a mild bellow.

The younger boys skimmed the ground like low-flying swallows. Everything passed by their senses in a blur—the image of the bull, the looming fence, and even the details of their young lives.

The city kid glanced backwards just once, for a split second. The picture he saw etched itself in his mind. It was almost as if a slow-motion movie camera was seeing the scene through his eyes. To this day he remembers every detail.

The ten-year-old picked up a chunk of wood and turned the tables on the bull. He brandished his puny club like a Viking with a battle-ax and let out as mighty a roar as his soprano voice permitted. There was nothing tentative about his charge—he headed for the holstein as fast as his brother and cousin fled.

The bull stopped short. He turned his big head sideways, staring incredulously at his opponent out of one black eye. He snorted again, this time with less self-confidence. The child screamed again. The bull backed up. The boy got closer.

Then the big animal raised his head and pivoted on his hind legs. With his eyes rolling in terror, he lurched for the open pasture.

The three boys walked slowly across the driveway to the

farmhouse and discussed the incident. The cousin was awe-struck.

"How did you do it?" he asked the ten-year-old.

"Oh, I wasn't worried," the hero said casually.

"But that bull could have killed us!"

"Naw," the farm boy said. "He doesn't know how big he is. We had him since he was a calf, and he still thinks he's a calf inside. He still thinks I could whup 'im."

The Case of the Missing Self-esteem

Too many of us are like the bull: We don't know our own strength or the resources at our command. When a bully shakes a fist at us or when somebody tries to shove us out to pasture, we turn tail and run. The Israelite spies whom we read about in the Old Testament (Numbers 13, 14) had God himself on their side. They had seen incredible miracles; they had felt the touch of God's protection and power; and they had partici-pated in a remarkable exodus from Egypt and through the des-ert. God had taken them to the very brink of a land flowing with milk and honey. If ever a group of people had reason to shout their confidence in God and march boldly to the land he had promised, it was the Israelites.

But just as they were about to enter the Promised Land, they found out about the giants. The Bible tells us the spies were so unnerved that they felt like grasshoppers in the presence of the big Canaanites. All their confidence dripped down to their shoes. The spies completely lost their sense of worth and power. They turned away in defeat. Instead of shouts, there were murmurs.

Years later, after God had firmly established the Israelites in the Promised Land, the sight of another bully turned them into cowards. The fellow's name was Goliath, and he made a show of challenging any Israelite to a fight. Not one of the children of God had the courage to stand up and say, "I'll handle this situation." Instead of shouts, there were whispers.

You remember the rest of the story. The shepherd boy,

David, finally came forward and volunteered to face the giant. The Bible doesn't tell us what David said on the morning of his fight with Goliath, but I'm sure he would have felt fairly comfortable, saying something like: "I feel healthy, I feel happy, I feel terrific!" The boy had so much confidence and self-esteem that he felt ten feet tall, and he marched into the world to do whatever needed to be done. He did so with vitality, commitment, and courage.

Too many people simply do not believe in themselves. Somehow Christians have confused self-confidence, self-acceptance, and self-esteem with pride, egoism, and self-centeredness. The Lord does not mix all those characteristics together in the same pot, though. In fact, he says, "You should love your God with all your heart, soul, and mind . . . and love your neighbor *as yourself*" (Matthew 22:37,39, *italics mine*).

The first three chapters of this book considered some of the key ways to love God with all your heart, mind, and soul through prayer, meditation, and solitude. Now we are going to examine how we can love our neighbors as ourselves. Together, we will explore an important trait found in our Christian faith, often called the *dignity of man.* We will focus especially on the dignity of oneself. This is more than a warm feeling or a key to successful living; it is another aspect of our journey into joy.

In 1 John 4:19 (KJV) we read, "We love him, because he first loved us." We are not sure—I believe—that we can subscribe to that statement. We love, because he loves. He loves us: Does he really? Why would he love you or me?

For years, society has explored history for insights. In recent years we have plumbed history's depths in a more scientific fashion. Research into the past discovers the evils of society, which have gone on through the centuries. We see scarcely a decade without a major war, people exploiting each other, and self-centeredness surfacing in most immoral ways. We do not feel very proud to be a part of the human race.

Those who document the news each night on television and those who write columns in our newspapers constantly remind us of the perversity of the human heart. There seems to be so little dignity in the actions of people who have power. Our national sports figures are no longer role models for our youngsters; judges make a mockery of justice; moviemakers constantly serve us a diet of hedonism and cheap thrills; and even a man in the Oval Office was seen to be more concerned with power politics than with personal integrity. We reach the point at which we wonder if anyone is worthy of our trust. The search for honest, upright leaders seems endless and futile.

Disgusted with what we see in the world, we explore our own inner depths. If we could just find something good inside our own psyches, then we could take heart. We study many schools of psychology and read books written by respected thinkers. Camus, the great existentialist writer, sums up this inner search in his book *The Fall*. He tells about Jean Baptiste Clamence, an attorney—a very successful man who is sympathetic to the needs of the poor—who ultimately looks within himself to discover his true motivations. What he discovers is vanity and violence. He finds nothing comforting and no answers. In the end he despairs.

"Worm Theology" Does Not Help Matters

The church has done much to destroy self-esteem. You may recall the lines in the hymn that say, "Would He devote that sacred head For such a worm as I?" The early American preacher Jonathan Edwards produced a well-known sermon along the same lines. In his graphic description of sinners in the hands of an angry God, we saw ourselves as loathsome insects. For years, the church said our view of ourselves as worms was laudable. We were worthless human beings simply hoping someday to be transformed. For most people, the transformation could not be expected until death and eternity.

The worm school of thought gives us little to inspire confidence or self-respect. True, our Christian faith must be clothed in an utter poverty of spirit. But when we take that truth out of context, it becomes the feeling of inferiority of a person who can scarcely accomplish enough in one lifetime to justify his existence.

No wonder so many Christians lose their self-respect! Why should God honor us when we fail him so often? Why should others esteem us? Why should we even respect ourselves? Sitting in the pew on a Sunday morning, putting on the appearance of dignity, we begin to feel like hypocrites.

Nobody really enjoys feeling like a worm—or worse yet, a hypocritical worm. So we attempt to do something about the situation. We set out to prove our worth. We try to appear to be strong and healthy. We find an identity in the successes of our children or in our family name or in our careers. We clutch at anything that will help us gain admiration. We want to make history, even if we need to break rules to gain notoriety. We crave recognition, popularity, meaningful titles. "I don't care what you say about me," the Hollywood star reputedly said to a gossip tabloid, "just so you get my picture on the front page."

Some people with money still build pyramids. Oh, they may not be the great stone edifices of Egypt, but they are structures designed to defy time—trusts, scholarships, institutions, or even cemetery monuments.

In our quest for self-worth, we sometimes identify with social groups that seem to be carving a niche in history. They play for immortality and recognition in the great sweep of human events. People in industry make their statements with strikes. Political action groups organize massive marches. Activists starve themselves or plant bombs. Buddhist monks set themselves on fire.

All social-action groups believe that they are motivated by a sense of right or justice. But I believe there is something even deeper. Napoleon made a statement, following the French Revolution, which seems to cut to the heart of the matter: "Vanity made the revolution," he said. "Liberty was only the pretext." I believe we can interpret Napoleon's word, *vanity,* to include a basic lack of self-esteem. People in France wanted to count for something. They wanted recognition. Madame

Defarge, sitting before the guillotine with her knitting, felt she was making a bold statement with her life.

Any young parent knows how disruptive a four-year-old can be when he feels he is being ignored. The little fellow would rather destroy a quiet afternoon, interrupt the conversation of his parents, and suffer painful consequences than lose his feeling of being an important little person. We grown-up children do similar things. We want to be recognized. We make some noise to prove our own worth. But if we sit back and reflect on what we're doing, perhaps with Camus's book in hand, we finally conclude, "So what? Does all the sound and fury signify nothing?"

We Look for Ourselves in the Wrong Places

Today, many of us are finding our world changed, with difficulties in business, problems with our families, loss of jobs, and disappointments in the future. We wonder where to go to find our identities. "Who are we?" we ask. We search, but in all the wrong places.

I wish to encourage you to find out who you are by helping you look in the right places. Too many people are so engrossed in making up for a lack of self-identity that they ignore the real basis of self-esteem. Their hunt goes on and on, but they are forever disappointed.

This quest has been going on in our society for a couple of decades. We constantly focus on self, self, self. We have become so egoistic that Christopher Lasch calls this "the age of look at ourselves—narcissism." Remember Narcissus in Greek mythology? The handsome young man looked down in a pool and saw his own reflection. His gaze was locked into the mirror image. Too vain and proud to love anyone else, he became so absorbed in his study of himself that eventually he pined away and lost his life.

Our society today repeats Narcissus's story. We are becoming so engrossed in our study of ourselves that we will perish from the egoism of our time. We're frozen above our own reflections.

Ironically, self-centeredness automatically destroys the very thing an egoist most needs: self-acceptance. *Self-absorption and self-acceptance are mutually exclusive.* We *never* find what we look for as long as we search within our own interests.

The way to personal affirmation leads *away* from the pool of Narcissus. Earlier in this chapter I referred to the two great commandments Christ gave his followers. The first is to love God, the second, to love your neighbor as yourself. Therein lies the answer. You cannot give what you do not possess. Possessed by self-love, you have no love to give. The way to find self-acceptance demands lifting your eyes up from your self-study, casting aside your quest for recognition, throwing down the blocks of your pyramid, forgetting your fear of being a worm, and relaxing in the arms of the Lord. If you depend on your job, your looks, your family name, or your accomplishments for feelings of self-worth, you eventually will gasp, "I feel *un*healthy, I feel *un*happy, I feel *terrible!*"

The Power of Self-Acceptance

We ought to give what we have and leave the results to God. We know by experience what that is. We ought not to *define* first who we are but, rather, to *accept* ourselves. No matter how small we think we are, we ought to find our calling. Harold Blake Walker tells a story about a piccolo player. She decided that it is really not much to play a piccolo. If you look over the scores of music, very little music requires a piccolo player. She sits most of the time listening to trumpets, violins, and drums, but she has just a little toot here and there. It does not mean that much to the orchestra. This musician decided that the orchestra could get along fine without her. During the concert she sat in her place, feeling glum, downhearted, and despondent. The orchestra, meanwhile, was playing. They arrived at the part of the score where there were notes for the piccolo player; she simply sat there, staring off into space. With this, the conductor became very upset. You can imagine him staring at someone who was not even looking at him.

Finally, during a crescendo in the playing, the conductor shouted so the audience could not hear, but the orchestra could, "Where is the piccolo player?" Suddenly, as she heard the desperation in the conductor's voice and realized that the entire orchestra was expecting her to perform her part that evening, the piccolo player recognized that she, too, was important. She felt, in that instant, the revelation of her place within the orchestra, and a new identity blossomed within her. She picked up her piccolo and played as never before!

Dr. Walker says he has never fogotten that no matter how small or seemingly unessential our place is, we ought to give what we have. However insignificant we may think the act—maybe a word or a smile, very little in the course of a week—we ought to give it. Nothing fantastic like a first-chair violin—just something back, out of sight, but nevertheless adding to the harmony of the whole. We ought to let the conductor decide when and what we play. If you're the kind of person who pins mottoes on the wall of your office or kitchen, you might consider having this slogan printed and framed: PICCOLO PLAYERS ARE IMPORTANT, TOO!

Finding out whether we're piccolo players, or flutists, or bass viol players is sometimes difficult—especially when events force us into positions far from where we expect to be.

The Bible Tells Us Who We Are

We often wrestle with the problem of identity. John says, "I will tell you who you are. You are a person whom God loves." If we truly believed that statement, we would respond to God's love by loving him in return. The statement "God loves you" is very simple. But like many simple things, it is filled with meaning.

By believing that we are people whom God loves, we rely less on our ability to control events and more on God's control over our events. Our ability to control things is nil anyway. No matter how much introspection we engage in, no matter how much time we spend thinking about the future, no matter how well our plans are laid, we do not run our lives.

In the Old Testament young Joseph learned the limits of his influence on events. He was sold into slavery, falsely accused of making sexual advances on the wife of his master, and then cast into prison—all while behaving in an upright, moral manner. This fine young man, with plans and dreams, saw everything slip out of his control. When God orchestrated the twists and turns in his young life, Joseph certainly had no idea where it all was leading. Not until much later in his life did he realize everything had a purpose.

The Bible tells us Jesus, in his human nature, also struggled with the purpose of his Father, although he never doubted the end results. In the Garden of Gethsemene, when Jesus asked God to change the way those purposes would be accomplished, he also said, "Nevertheless, not my will, but yours be done."

What a strange way our own lives unfold! When I was a college student, I knew that the last place on earth that I ever wanted to live was the Chicago area. There are many nice parts of the city and many lovely suburbs around it, but my view of the city, suburbs, and anything between them, was colored by a childhood experience collecting garbage in the heart of the city.

As a youngster I had a friend whose father was in the refuse business. His collection routes covered the heart of Chicago. On different occasions I traveled to that area from my home in Michigan and helped my friend and his father with their routes. I rode the trains into Chicago and formed part of my opinion of the whole area from what I saw through the train windows. The train tracks, of course, followed the backs of tenements and factories.

Then, at five o'clock each morning I drove up and down the alleys around Clark and Madison Streets, picking up garbage and pitching it into a truck. Rats ran around our boots; drunks slept in doorways. To my young mind that was the Chicago area. I wanted no part of it.

Several years later I graduated from seminary. Where do you think I went to serve my first congregation? That's right—the Chicago area! I have stayed here more than thirty years now, and I am pleased to call it my home. In fact, I would not even consider leaving this dynamic, multifaceted heartland of the country! Someone wiser than me knew that the best route for my life would lead back to Chicago.

Of course, my story is not unique. You may have had similar experiences. If so, you know from your own life that we are not in charge of our own destiny. To think that we are is a delusion that produces much agony, insecurity, and self-centeredness. To understand that our loving Father in heaven controls our lives leads to peace and self-assurance.

Only God Is Great

The God who loves us is a God of great power and strength. Really, in the earth's catalog of movers and shakers, God is *the* only One who is great.

Louis XIV of France (1638–1715) certainly occupies some space in the catalog of great men. During his life, the Sun King received godlike honor and power. When he died, it was only fitting that he should be buried in the most famous religious edifice in his country: Notre Dame Cathedral.

The notables of Europe gathered there, properly attired in all their finery. Remember: It was an age of pageantry. The splendidly bedecked visitors sat in the cathedral, ready for the eulogy of the priest, expecting him to tell them what a marvelous man Louis XIV had been. The priest mounted his pulpit and looked out over that very prestigious audience. Then he said, "Only God is great." Like cold steel, this cut into the hearts of those assembled as they suddenly sobered in a great hush. Imagine what that meant. All this pomp and show would dissolve into a wooden box like the one sitting in their midst. Finally, that which was inside the box would return to the dust of the earth. That priest reminded everyone present of a truth no one should ever forget: ONLY GOD IS GREAT.

It is the same for you and me, my friend. If we expect to find reason to believe in our importance, we are mistaken. We will not find it on earth. We are all mortal. Whatever we have and whatever we are is not enough to give us self-esteem. It may collapse in a moment. And if it does, we have lost everything.

Jesus told a parable about two men who built homes. One built on sand, the other on rock. The man whose house was built on sand found that when the storms came, with the winds and rushing waters, his house would not stand fast. He lost everything. If you base your esteem on material things—things that are so quickly gone—it can be so quickly lost. But this need not happen. For the God who is great also loves you when you do not desire it and have done nothing to merit it. We need to learn that God provides the solid rock in our lives. On that support we can build secure lives, knowing that they will withstand the ravages of life's storms. Like the rock waiting for someone to build upon it, God is waiting for you and me to build upon him. He wants us to receive him. He wants to be our firm foundation.

To Build Without God Is Folly

We need God's love as the basis for our lives. Walter Trobisch tells the story of the young man who came to him with a great concern. He had overheard a conversation between his parents many years before, in which he discovered he was an unwanted child. That thought kept going through his mind and haunting him. He was unwanted. The more people who rejected him, the more he began to suspect that others did not welcome his presence. He increasingly realized how unloved he had been until, in exasperation, he was ready to end his life.

Walter chose a roundabout way of showing the young man that his predicament was not unique. He described a situation, in fact, in which a young man had been in even worse straits and yet accomplished great things for God. Could the young man think of any other men in history who had been "unwanted"? Could he think of one who had been born to an unmarried girl? Could he imagine the pain in the heart of this man's mother when she had to explain her pregnancy to her fiancé and others in her community?

Those circumstances, of course, surrounded the birth of God's own Son. In the first part of his ministry, he was a man unwanted by people in his home district. They took him to a high cliff with the intent of pushing him to his death. He later was unwanted by his country's leaders, rejected by a populace that didn't understand his mission, and even denied by one of his closest disciples. After he was nailed to a cross, this same Son of God called out to his own Father, "My God, My God, why have you forsaken me?"

Walter Trobisch asked his young friend if Jesus had ever felt unwanted—even though Jesus had God's blessing and full support. The young man began to understand that God's leading wasn't a safeguard against negative feelings. Even God's own Son felt disapproval and rejection.

The important thing to remember was that God cared, and in his power he ordered the events of the young man's life. If he truly believed that, he could overcome any feelings of rejection with the same kind of self-esteem Jesus must have had as he did his Father's will.

There Is One Who Understands

As you struggle with loneliness, someone totally understands. He loves you with compassion and understanding. Because God so cared for us, he gave his own "unwanted" Son. The servant is not above his Lord; rather, the servant can find the same strength that his Lord found. Jesus' greatness rests not in the recognition given him by Pilate, by the Pharisees, by his contemporaries, or by anyone else who lived. The greatness of Jesus is found in the love of the Father. We share an equal opportunity to experience that love because he first loved us and we turn to him in love.

As we explore the steps we can take in our journey into joy

let us begin with this basic understanding: Before we can love one another, we must love others as God loves us. I believe one of the greatest sins is to have such low self-esteem that you deny God's love for you. Not accepting his love is one thing, but not allowing it to flow within you and through you also becomes a form of denial.

Can you accept God's love? Can you open your heart to him? Can you let him pour his love into you? Go into the world knowing that you are what he wants you to be. It is the way he made you. A mark of true spirituality is understanding that God loves you. Like the piccolo player in the orchestra or Joseph in Egypt, you receive duties and abilities from your loving God, and he knows exactly how you can best serve him. We use the following, very appropriate phrase often: "What you are is God's gift to you; what you become is your gift to God."

Study Questions

1. Discuss the conflict of views many Christians have held on the subjects of self-esteem and poverty of spirit. What has the church done to help or hinder a right view of this issue? How can Christians properly balance these in their lives?
2. The author says, "Self-absorption and self-acceptance are mutually exclusive." Why is this true? What forms the *real* basis for self-acceptance?
3. What does God say about us? What should our response be? How can we show this in our lives?
4. What is the difference between self-confidence and pride? Are there biblical illustrations of each?

5

Simplicity: Avoiding Life's Complexities

But seek ye first the kingdom of God, and his righteousness; and
all these things shall be added unto you.
Matthew 6:33 (KJV)

Have you ever felt trapped by the complexities of life? Is there never quite enough time to accomplish everything? Do you wish every day held another few hours and that someone could add another day to the week? You have problems sorting out what you ought to do and how you ought to do it. Let's stop and analyze why this has happened by considering the discipline of simplicity.

A number of things cause the busyness of life, among them, many of our own desires. Your wants reflect what you are trying to find in life. They describe what you look for—your expectations—those things that define life's success or failure. You reach out for the acceptance of others. You want people to like you and accept you. In the process, you have to be careful that you do things that will not offend.

In the last chapter we talked about being wanted, especially by God. Your relationship with God has a large impact on your self-esteem. In this chapter we will explore how strong self-esteem can help you to simplify your life.

I heard recently about a poll that was taken to rate the performance of the president. When pollsters asked Americans how they felt the president was doing, only 38 percent approved. That is not enough. So the implication is that the president must conform more to their expectations. Then people will accept him. Unlike the president, we are not running for office, but for some reason we still act as if we are. We try to do those things people will notice and admire, because we crave acceptance. So we conform with our clothing and our schedules. We want to do a little bit of everything, and we become aware of our lack of time. We try the most popular sport, or we try to please with the acceptance of dates and appointments. We go places we do not enjoy. We spend money for things we are not interested in, to impress people we do not really care about. We crave acceptance. Even in unfamiliar places, we wonder what strangers think of us as we walk by. That causes a bit of unrest in our lives.

These complexities entrap us for another reason—we have joined in the search for pleasure. Told by others to pursue happiness and joy, we work hard at indulging ourselves. Because power and popularity make us feel good, we want to gain them. We secure possessions—all those *things* that make life wonderful. The media and advertising bombard us with pitches that build our desire for houses, vacations, jewelry, stylish clothing, automobiles, and all the rest.

It takes hours to discover the just-right automobile or the perfect personal computer system. We spend an enormous amount of time on the search. When we find what we want, we often do not have enough money to pay for it. That creates another problem. But these material things—always a few more than we have—are so necessary! We want to appear successful; we want admiration. People ought to look at us and say, "Isn't he great! Isn't she something?"

Perhaps there is one more thing that we want: security. We seek security for ourselves and for our children. We look at the future, and it seems so uncertain and foreboding. We worry about what will happen to all the things we have accumulated. We feel compelled to spend a great deal of time and money being sure we have secured our possessions. We use dead bolts, alarms, insurance, security guards, and even fierce dogs—all to make sure no one takes them from us. Concern about the things that guard our things adds to our busyness. We become distracted and torn.

This concern is not new in our generation. Even more than a thousand years ago, getting ahead in life was difficult, and many kinds of pressures created complex tensions. Thoughtful Christians at that time were as concerned about the situation as we are in the modern age. Those believers wanted to get back to a purer form of Christianity. They felt that simplicity was best—and they thought they could achieve it by founding monasteries. The monastic movement sprang from a desire to uncomplicate life and simply serve God.

Thomas Merton writes, "Society was regarded by the desert fathers as a shipwreck from which each individual man had to swim for his life." So the Eastern founders of this system went to the desert, built their monasteries, and claimed the simple way of life. They rejected society and all its materialistic, busy complications. We know this brings about no solution.

This is God's world! He does not call us to flee from it. He wants us to be in it and part of it—the salt of it, the light of it, the yeast of it. We must face the challenge of being in it but not of it. We wrestle with the busyness and the problems of allocating our time and interests. At the same time we struggle to be released from fear, guilt, and frustration. How can we overcome all this?

Simplicity Does Not Mean Being Simplistic

Simplicity holds the answer. I am not talking about being simplistic. It is like watching an organist play the organ. If you ever really watched, it looks easy. All the organist does is skip his feet around on the pedals and his hands on the keyboards, and marvelous music comes out. Try it yourself. It becomes easy when you have practiced and mastered the art. But playing this instrument is extremely difficult for a beginner. At first nothing seems to go right. You feel awkward and clumsy. The same rule applies with spiritual disciplines. Don't be surprised to find that simplicity is not very simple. You must develop this inner disposition.

I am not going to give you a time-management seminar or talk about a set of rules prescribing what you do and when you do it. And I am not going to tell you how to keep your notebook or whatever you use to schedule yourself. I want to talk to you about something inside yourself—your thoughts, attitudes, disposition. We are going to think together about how we ought to perceive life.

The Attitude Behind Simplicity

Simplicity is something we like to talk about, but we often don't know how to accomplish. We have a feeling that finding it isn't as easy as chopping off hunks of our lives or ranking all the elements of our existence on a value scale of one to fifty and never getting a chance to pay attention to items at the bottom of the list. *No*—there's something else involved in finding simplicity, something self-help books and weekend seminars can't give us.

Jesus put his finger on the elusive quality of simplicity when he described it as an *attitude,* not a *state.* He gave us an excellent outline for developing that attitude in Matthew 6—part of the Sermon on the Mount. First he talked about simplicity, about the attitude we ought to have toward the disciplines of life. He began by saying, in that chapter, "If you are going to give your alms—if you are going to make donations to the church and to the kingdom—do so quietly and in secret. Enjoy what you are doing in a very private, personal way. Do not look for the accolades of others, for then you will have one kind of reward. It is much better to find the reward of your heavenly Father." Jesus built upon the Old Testament idea of giving. We need to look back and see how it was done.

Abraham was the first giver. In Genesis 14 we read about his unusual military campaign to rescue his nephew, Lot, from a victorious army led by four kings; they had swept into Lot's area, defeated the local army, and carried off food, goods, and captives. The victory of the marauding rulers was complete. Abraham assembled a force of about three hundred men, fell on the victorious army at night, and recovered all the captives and booty.

When he returned with the treasures, Abraham displayed a remarkable lack of interest in filling his own purse with the just rewards of his campaign. He met a priest named Melchizedek and gave a tenth of the spoils to him. Then he gave all that was left back to the king of Sodom! Abraham returned home with nothing but the satisfaction of knowing that he had saved Lot and his family and had done a tremendous service for the people in and around Sodom. What price would any other desert chieftain have exacted for that kind of service? Fifty percent? Eighty percent? Retention of the most valuable treasures?

All Abraham did was devote 10 percent to the Lord. The idea of tithing was born.

Tithing appears a number of times in the Old Testament. Turn to Deuteronomy 14, where Moses gave his people the law concerning their giving. He points out that the people should give their tithes to the Levites, the religious leaders of the day, for the care of the tabernacle and later the temple. Their tithe would also pay for the expenses of the religious ceremonies, for the care of the poor and aged, and for great religious holidays. Giving was to be a joyous event, not something done begrudgingly without any thought of the pleasure of giving.

Jesus reflected this idea, saying we should give quietly and enjoy what we are doing. It should not provoke guilt or fear. He goes on to say that giving, like prayer and fasting, should be done in secret, before our Father, who sees in secret and who will reward each of us in secret. How many people give only when coerced by their friends or to join the "big-hitters club"? Fund raisers appeal to such motives. Jesus made it very simple. You make the decision. You are accountable only to God. Be yourself. As you practice your Christian life, be sure you set your priorities straight. Think about the things you regard as your treasures—the things in life that you really care for. Your home, hobbies, business, social standing, or dreams for your children. How much time and effort do you put into developing these treasures?

"Do not store up for yourselves treasures on earth. . . ," Jesus tells us in the Sermon on the Mount. "But store up for yourselves treasures in heaven . . ." (Matthew 6:19, 20 NIV). Where you spend your time leads you back to your treasure.

I know of a country preacher who spent thirty years serving small, struggling congregations in states such as South Dakota and Montana. That sincere, quiet fellow devoted his life to his people and family. Financially, he found every dollar of his meager income spirited away by the costs of raising his family and paying for their unusually high medical bills. He enjoyed his work and watched his children grow up to be productive members of society. A few years ago, a relative of the preacher died and left him an unexpectedly large inheritance.

It was instructive to see how the man reacted to the sudden deluge of money. He had never owned his own home, and he considered investing in real estate that would become his retirement home. He considered dabbling in reliable stocks and bonds. He began thinking about tax shelters. One of his sons recommended a "sure thing" in a stock purchase that was a bit more speculative. He began spending time each evening with interest tables and a calculator.

Then this preacher realized that the inheritance was occupying more and more of his time. He began to feel it was taking the fine edge off a ministry that was remarkably well focused and simple. At that point he decided to put the money in bank certificates of deposit—and nothing more. His own response to the situation was to opt for the simplest possible maintenance of the money. I'm sure he also donated sums to charitable causes, and with the bulk of the inheritance he chose simplicity over high financial rewards. The man still serves small churches, as he always has done.

In Matthew 6:21 (KJV), Jesus says, "For where your treasure is, there will your heart be also." I'm sure many people are able to play the stock market without regarding it as their heart's treasure. But there is always a danger in spending too much time with things, possessions, treasures. Jesus advises us to lay up for ourselves *real* treasures, where there is no corruption, no looting, no risk of loss, and no deterioration.

Jesus emphasized that our security is in our heavenly Father. Do not forget it. You will not find security on earth. If you have a sense of security in God, then all things will take care of themselves. He summarizes it all in Matthew 6:33 by saying, "But seek ye first the kingdom of God. . . ." Seek it. Desire it. Want it. Crave it. Go after it. Aggressively find the kingdom. It will not come to you if you lie back in your recliner and wait for it. You need to seek and ask. Then it will be given.

Your search should not be a spare-time effort. If you are serious in your pursuit, you will need to devote your best energies to the effort. Make it number one on your daily priority list. The Bible says that the kingdom is like a pearl of great price for which you would give anything if you could possess it. If you have that kind of attitude, you will find what you seek.

Knowing if God Is Pleased

We have covered a great number of points in this chapter. Jesus focuses our minds on one thing: his kingdom. We must answer the question: Is God pleased with what we are doing? The kingdom of God is not a geographic thing. It does not and will not exist in Jerusalem. We do not look for it one day in the distant future. The kingdom, Christ has told us, is within. It is the power of God in your heart. Does God really rule within you? When he does, all these other things fall into place.

What do you think was the real moving force in the life of

Jesus? What made him so great? Why do you follow him? There is only one answer: He did the Father's will. It was his chief concern. He did exactly what he tells us to do. He sought his Father's will. That is a very essential, basic thing. If we can keep our lives that simple, we take care of all our complexities.

Let me give you an example. Richard Foster talks about the distribution of time that results from removing the complexities in your life. He tells us that each of us is a conglomerate of many selves. A civic self expresses interest in the community and does volunteer work. Then the vocational self concentrates on the things needed in a profession or trade. There is the family self, with obligations to your spouse, your children, your parents, brothers, and sisters—the extended family. The educational self wants to learn and to grow and develop. Finally the religious self needs to pray, to meditate, to fast, to go to classes, and to attend church. All of these selves vie for time.

You decide on a particular night to sit home, put your feet up by the fire, listen to Chopin on the stereo, and look through some of those magazines you have not seen for a while. Your energetic self does not want you to sit like that. Your civic self says, "You ought to be out working on that committee." Your religious self says, "You ought to go to church or go to that religion class." Your family self says, "You ought to be helping the children with their studies." Naturally you become distressed and uneasy. The question needs to be answered, must be answered, by some higher being. You need a divine arbiter, someone to settle all this for you.

I was very thankful one day when I read a little book by Charlie Shedd, *Time for All Things,* on how to spend time. He pointed out that Jesus walked away from the crowds on occasion, indicating he did not have time for them at that point. He also made it clear that he needed to go to a quiet place to rest and pray. And he simply left them. There is a time when we need to say no to things with a clear conscience, not being accountable to anyone else. Knowing how Jesus responded to demands on his time is very helpful.

Steps to Achieving Simplicity

We need to decide what God wants from us. What does he desire in our lives? That is the only important question. Then everything else will fall into place. Whether or not someone approves means very little once we know God approves. If we could destroy all the pressures facing us, how simple life could become. It would fall naturally into the proper perspective. We would have many things to accomplish, but we would not do them with such complex feelings, pressure, and sometimes even guilt. We must understand that we can say no to things. God has told us to get our priorities straight and then stick to them.

How do you do this? First, focus on God. Be centered on him. Practice prayer, meditation, and solitude, which will focus your mind on God. Second, be controlled by God, not by anyone else. Someone invites you to take on a project, and you try to persuade him that you really should not and cannot. That is not necessary. Silence alone is necessary when you have made a decision for God. You account to God for your works, to no one else. You need not manipulate someone else's opinion of you. Do not concern yourself with another's opinion of your action. Are you doing God's will? Let him control your life.

Likewise avoid controlling someone else. Sometimes we unintentionally indulge in this common habit. Parents lay guilt on their children for not fulfilling selfish and unnecessary demands. I recently dealt with a woman in her mid-forties who lost her husband before she realized that she was being manipulated by her father. I'm sure the father didn't mean to destroy his daughter's happiness. We need to be sensitive to the integrity of those we influence.

Third, obey without asking any reason of God. When you know he wants you to do something, simply do it. He is not accountable to you. You do not have to understand the future. Be like Jesus in Gethsemane when he told his heavenly Father that he did not want to follow his Father's express wishes but that he would do so because God had told him to. No matter how distasteful it is or how unreasonable it seems, if God says to do it, then do it.

Fourth and last, pick yourself up when you fall. Do not stay down and enjoy being there. "Poor me! Look what happened. I need your sympathy. I need your attention." Get on your feet, accept forgiveness, refocus, and start again. This is simplicity. Focus on God: on his kingdom, on his righteousness, and on his will.

Study Questions

1. Name some attitudes and actions that keep us from finding simplicity in our lives. How did Abraham and the preacher seek to simplify their lives?
2. What did Jesus say about simplicity? What were the real treasures he spoke about?
3. Name the four steps you can take to get your priorities straight with God. How can you tell what pleases him?
4. What single word would best describe the desire of your life? Are you making progress toward your goal? How does your quest fit into the practice of simplicity?

6

Fasting: Using Your Secret Weapon

. . . Your father, who sees what is done in secret, will reward you.
Matthew 6:18 (NIV)

As we have seen, we sometimes do amazing things because of peer pressure. If we are not careful, we will build our lives under pressure. At times like these, we *need* to be checked out by someone or some group, but the Christian life must not always be based on what others think or say.

A complex aspect of the Christian's journey into joy, one that takes much self-discipline, is the realm of those things done alone and in secret. Here some worthwhile things of life are conceived and done. Meaningful spiritual acts, covenants between man and God and man and himself take place within. Only within himself can the addict make the final decision to deny himself that addicting substance. You alone know your private feelings toward others, feelings you may never have confided in another human being.

Secret things *do* matter, however unpopular they may be. The private, hard-to-comprehend parts of our personalities

97

and characters require depth of perception. Sometimes that which we confess in sincerity in the presence of God will be ignored in our daily lives. The desire to do right and subsequent wrong actions may exist together. That conflict takes place in the solitary places of the soul.

Jesus practiced an inner life consistent with its external expression. His disciples saw that and asked him to teach them how to live as he did. One of the insights Jesus gave them concerned fasting. Of it, he said in Matthew 6:18, ". . . Your father, who sees what is done in secret, will reward you." Jesus was recommending a solitary spiritual discipline that can grip and change the human soul.

Why Fasting Is Not Popular Today

We generally avoid fasting because it is a private, secret practice. We are a people who need public affirmation. The founder of Weight Watchers has said that the only reason Weight Watchers succeeds is because of peer pressure. That pressure comes to bear on the person who must get on the scale in the presence of the whole class and be accountable for having done or not having done what he was supposed to do. People could lose weight privately, but they do not.

Fasting is not very American. We love to eat. A considerable number of prosperous establishments are built on this habit. To be able to go out to eat and be able to eat exactly what you want to eat are probably some of the first expressions of success for the middle class. How many gourmet clubs have formed around the country in recent years? We like to eat, and we suffer all the consequences.

I think another reason we are not really happy about fasting in this country is because we like to be free. We want to do what we want, whenever we want to do it. And we do whatever feels good. You may have seen the bumper sticker IF IT FEELS GOOD, DO IT. Just once, I would like to run into the back of a car with that slogan. When the driver jumps out of the car and asks me why I ran into him, I would say, "Because it feels good."

What Exactly Is Fasting?

Who wants to fast? Fasting does not feel good at all. Rather, we might describe it as a discipline of distaste, something we find hard to do, difficult to continue, and that requires self-denial. We do not find this practice either pleasant or enjoyable; yet it can significantly enhance our spiritual growth.

Fasting requires our limiting or completely denying the intake of food, drink, or both, for a period of time. It is done with a desire for some accomplishment. Its significance is in what you do with it. However, recognize that if you fast, you will benefit physically. There is no doubt that for the average, healthy person fasting results in good health. It cleanses the system.

Not all fasts give such spectacular results, and some physical ailments preclude a complete fast, but a surgeon in Detroit reported on the consequences of his experience. The article appeared in the *Chicago Tribune,* in 1977, in the Food Guide, of all places. The topic was "The Body at Rest." The man's health had been deteriorating, and finally a series of tests gave him the dread diagnosis—impending death. He reacted by periodic fasting. Many months passed, and his health seemed to improve. More tests. Finally the tests showed that the cure was complete. The surgeon believes that regular fasting so cleansed his digestive, circulatory, nervous, and other systems, that he came out of the ordeal with a new body.

In addition to the physical value, fasting has great spiritual value. Did you know that Isaiah 58 is entirely devoted to the subject of fasting? This chapter of the Bible describes how fasting can become an abuse. Do you remember the story of Jesus discussing those who fasted twice a week? They would put on the proper garments and the long, sober face of suffering and stand on the busiest corners of the street. While all the other people went to market, they passed the fasters on the street corners. Bypassers would comment on how pious these men were. Jesus said, "They have their reward."

There is nothing honorable about a public display of spiritual discipline. In fact, if anything irritated Jesus, it was the thought that somehow you could impress God with physical or material things or with external disciplines. God does not honor external things. He looks at the heart. It is what Joel the prophet meant when he told the people to rend their hearts, not their garments. Anyone can tear up his garments and say, "Look at how I am suffering." God wants to see you humble before him as the sovereign One. He blesses and strengthens your quiet, secret commitment.

The Only Reason to Fast

True fasting is another aspect of our journey into joy. You make this a very secret, voluntary, personal commitment, with a desire to grow in your faith. If you want to deepen your spiritual life, deny yourself food and drink. That process of denial will bring rich benefits.

I do not mean to imply that food and drink are wrong. In fact, in many ways after a fast they taste much better. Fasting does not involve moral choice. Choosing not to eat does not equal choosing right from wrong. It is simply a voluntary discipline. If you are on medication or if you have other physical conditions in your life that are not normal, please get your physician's approval or prescription before you try fasting.

I assure you that, if you fast, you will know it. You will experience heightened awareness every hour, every minute of your fast. You will feel hungry. You will be thirsty. Nobody else will know it, but you will know it. It is all inside, and every time you think about food or drink you will think about the fact that you are doing this as a means to come closer to God. Your discipline will have its reward.

Members of my congregation have told me that they find it difficult to think about anything but food while they fast. For them, it requires additional discipline to refocus their thoughts on God. When you deny yourself something, whether you choose food or drink or something else, be sure you will miss it. You are probably most familiar with the mini-fasts that are assumed by individuals in Lent. They remind the fasting person of the suffering of Jesus. Unfortunately, however, many do not take the Lenten fast seriously. I had a man tell me once that during Lent he was going to give up something. When I asked what, he replied, "I have denied myself something; I am not going to swim in Lake Michigan during Lent." That was great self-denial! We laugh and say to ourselves, "Boy, did he miss the point!" As you reflect on what you can give up in fasting, make it something that you will miss. Let it remind you *constantly,* throughout your fast, of Christ's suffering for our sins.

Believers Have Always Fasted

Christians fast as a reminder of their goals of spirituality and growth. This is nothing new, but is a Christian tradition as old as the call of God. In Old Testament times, fasting was a part of life. David wrote in Psalm 35, ". . . I humbled myself with fasting. . . ." In Leviticus 16, when the law regarding the Day of Atonement was given, that day was called a day of fasting. On that great day the High Priest went into the Holy of Holies—on behalf of the people—to bring God a sacrifice representing the repentant, humble spirit of the people.

In later times, when Luke wrote about fasting, recorded in Acts 27, he called it the fast day. In the Old Testament writings, Ezra called fasts at the time of the reconstruction of Jerusalem and of the temple. Esther called a seventy-two-hour fast when her people stood in jeopardy because of the edict of the king. The people of Nineveh fasted and prayed because they wanted to find favor in the sight of God. They were honored for their acts. It gripped them in such a way that their spiritual lives were not only reinforced but rechanneled.

Illustrations of fasting appear all through the Scriptures. Moses practiced fasting; so did Elijah, Nehemiah, and Isaiah. The New Testament carries many stories of fasting. Jesus abstained forty days, you remember, when he prepared himself for his ministry. Anna was fasting when she held the Christ child. In the context of life, Jesus said, "When you fast. . . ." It was a habit, a part of the curriculum of the faithful. Before Saul and Barnabas began their missionary travels, they fasted with the church. In this context of fasting, the mission program was conceived and born. You can trace this spiritual practice down through history to the time of Bernard of Clairvaux and the church fathers and to Calvin, Luther, Knox, Wesley, and the Reformers.

When the king of England decided to place an embargo against Boston, starting on June 1, 1774, the House of Burgesses in Virginia passed a resolution that June 1 was to be a day of prayer, humility, and fasting. We read in the diary of George Washington for June 1, 1774: "I attended church and fasted all day." Later John Adams and James Madison declared national fasts in this country—fasts accompanied by prayer and humility before God—as did Abraham Lincoln during the Civil War. You see, it is part of our national spiritual heritage. Yet we say very little about it.

The Benefits of Fasting

Fasting is a blessing that draws you closer to God. How can you help but be attracted to him with this constant reminder? Share your secret with no one. Feel privately in your innermost self that you are reaching out with new dedication because you really want to be closer to God. As you do, you will begin to understand yourself a little better. You will separate what is important from what you thought was important. You will begin to comprehend what makes you tick, your moods, your feelings, your attitude, because the more time you spend with God the less proficient you will be at making excuses. You will find that God will strengthen, stabilize, and balance your life.

Fasting cannot be undertaken without a serious commitment and a desire to see your fast through to its conclusion. I remember my first experience. I decided not to eat for twenty-four hours. My quest was to gain a greater awareness of the presence of God and his love for me. I decided that I would drink only water, but not eat. The first few hours were easy. But as the day passed I became very hungry. I found that I really *wanted* food! I asked myself over and over, "Have I ever desired the presence of God as much as I now desire food?" This hard question persisted long after the fast ended.

Fasting forced me to ask that question and to come face-to-face with myself with new honesty. After all, I had voluntarily decided to fast, and my intention was to deepen my spiritual life. To give myself a phony answer in response to the question of my desiring God as much as I desired food seemed doubly deceptive. I would deceive God and myself! I had no intent to waste my time by kidding myself with less than an honest conclusion to my concern. The process of thinking this through provided an introduction to a new spiritual discipline in my life. That profound experience set me on a new spiritual adventure.

You are probably asking yourself, "But how did he deal with the constant hunger?" I resolved that each and every time hunger gripped me I would use it to remind me of my quest for a greater awareness of the presence of God. I chose also to remember God's love for me. Each time I felt the pain of hunger, I forced myself to focus my thoughts on the pain Jesus Christ suffered for my sins. It taught me a great deal about God's love. In this way, I put the distractions of hunger and hunger pains to a positive use in the time of fast. I felt a renewed strength and balance as a result of this experience.

Along with new strength and balance will come a new power of intercession. In Psalm 35, David said he prayed and fasted for his enemies. Isaiah also tells us to fast for others. An article in *Guideposts* told how John Stanton—a minister in Massachusetts—decided to put this into practice. He took literally the word of Jesus to his disciples when they came to him and asked why they could not do what he was doing. He replied that he was able to do the things he did because of prayer and fasting. Based on this story, Reverend John Stanton started to fast for other people. He tells about an alcoholic who kept coming to him but always fell back into the drinking habit.

Stanton finally said, "I am all through talking to you. I am going to fast for you." The alcoholic looked at him rather strangely!

Reverend Stanton has had astounding results through the years. When he finds that people are in the grip of something devastating, evil, and difficult, he fasts for them. Stanton asks nothing of those for whom he fasts. He does make them aware of what he is doing. He testifies to the enormous power of intercessory fasting. People really understand what caring means when you are willing to discipline yourself while they indulge themselves. The power inherent in fasting not only produces a sense of self-control, it creates confidence in the Lord. It defeats pride because it is based on humility.

I invite you to try fasting, if you have not already done so. One of the most common practices is a twenty-four-hour fast every week. Just as you worship each week, have a spiritually oriented fast one day a week. You will be amazed at what will happen in your life. But it must be done quietly, secretly. Your spouse, perhaps, will know, but no one else. "And the Father," Jesus says, "who sees what you do in secret, will reward you."

Study Questions

1. Why is what is done in private important to the journey into joy? Including concepts from previous chapters, describe ways Christians can foster this personal aspect of their relationship with God.
2. Why is fasting the Christian's secret weapon? What attitudes are essential to a successful fast? Why do people avoid fasting?
3. Consider some of the blessings of fasting. What are the biblical precedents for doing this? What were some of the results of these fasts?
4. Did you ever think of fasting as a method of finding God's will regarding a specific decision? Do you know of anyone who has?

Part III

Journey Into Deeper Faith

7

Faith: Believing Without Fear

But without faith it is impossible to please him. . . .
Hebrews 11:6 (KJV)

Two hundred boys participated in a wilderness camp experience a few years ago. As often happens in survival-type camps, two of the boys in attendance became fast friends. One was tall and athletic and an experienced camper. We'll call him Jeff. The other was exactly the opposite—he was stubby and uncoordinated, and he attended the camp mainly to please his parents. We'll call him Matt. The boys paired off as they liked and attended workshops in nature lore, wilderness survival skills, and self-reliance in stress situations. Jeff acted as the leader; Matt depended on him "to stay in one piece until we get back to civilization."

All the campers studied orienteering. The rugged terrain around the campsite provided a perfect setting for lessons about the compass and map reading. The boys learned how to take a bearing and then follow it through thick brush and across steep-sided ravines. Every day different groups of campers rotated through the training session and then tested their new skills on a tough, four-hour course. Timekeepers kept track of each pair of boys who ran the course, and the highest marks were to be made public on the last night of camp, Recognition Night. The campers responded to the competitive arrangement by running like a pack of wolves from point to point on the course.

The two friends went through the session together. They were completely mismatched as far as their abilities to perform well on the course. Not only did Jeff excel at such a strenuous activity, but he had studied some books on orienteering before coming to camp. Matt became more and more confused as the training session progressed. When the instructor explained declination, adjusting a compass reading to account for magnetic north, Matt realized that the only way he'd get through the day would be to put his faith in his better-oriented friend.

The run through the course started as a group affair. The boys paired off, and each pair received a compass, map, checklist, and instruction sheet. A dozen pairs of boys ran the course at the same time, and when the starting gun exploded, they all took off at a gallop in the same direction.

The first markers were relatively easy to find, and the boys stayed together. After a half hour some of the faster pairs forged ahead, and the slower ones began to lag behind. Some boys made mistakes and had to backtrack to find the course. Each pair increasingly depended on individual decisions, rather than the consensus of the pack. Runners began to string out and lose sight of each other on the course.

Matt felt hard pressed to keep up with the group, but Jeff dragged him along. As the pack fell apart, Matt started unhesitatingly to depend on the decisions of his buddy. "A hundred and twenty paces toward the dead tree," Jeff would say, and Matt would recap his canteen and take off behind him.

On they went, crashing through undergrowth and climbing up and down rocks. At times, a direction that Jeff figured out would seem impossible, but they always managed to stumble upon the next marker in the general vicinity of his calculations. As the afternoon wore on, Matt even began to understand how Jeff got his bearings and made his calculations. (Declination, however, remained a mystery to him.)

As they hit the eighteenth marker, they knew they were making fairly good time. They hadn't made any serious errors. They could not know if they were in the lead, but guessed that they must be pretty close. All they had left was marker number nineteen, and then the run to the last point on the course.

Then Jeff and Matt heard voices ahead of them on the way to number nineteen. Four boys were ahead of them on the course! Their jog through the pine trees became a lung-bursting run. Matt watched his buddy gain on the leaders and called up reserves of energy he never knew he had. All six boys converged on number nineteen at the same time. It was on a low hill just outside the camp. A dirt trail led from the marker down to the headquarters tent at the campsite. The boys took their bearings quickly and dashed full speed down the hill toward the tent—all the boys, that is, except Jeff and Matt.

"Something's wrong," Jeff said as he looked up from his compass to his friend. "No matter how I figure it, I get a beeline toward that thicket, not back to the camp. Would they put the last marker in a bush on the backside of this hill?"

Matt looked at the instructions. "Sure doesn't look right," he agreed. "You got us this far, though. Lead the way!"

So down the other side of the hill they went, crashing through the bushes.

You can guess the end of the story. An instructor with a sense of humor had indeed plotted the final leg of the orienteering course in a direction that few boys would take unless they were very sure of themselves. The final marker was located on the other side of the thicket, and Jeff and Matt earned one of the top scores on the course.

The story of the two boys in the wilderness gives us a little insight into the meaning of *faith*. Faith is difficult to explain in hard, cold language—it always is related to an experience or a relationship. An understanding of true faith comes from an understanding of your relationship with God. On a human scale, we all are like Matt, depending on a stronger, wiser friend to keep us going on life's racecourse.

Two verses from the Bible introduce our exploration of this

part of spiritual life. We find the first in Hebrews 11:6 (KJV): "But without faith it is impossible to please him. . . ." I think you recognize the integral part that faith plays in your spiritual life—from faith in simple little things to faith in God's divine plan as it pertains to major undertakings and directions.

The second verse is found in Mark 9:24: ". . . Lord, I believe; help thou mine unbelief." This verse points toward our need to grow in faith. We believe, but we want to work on the nagging, gnawing unbelief that undermines our journey into joy. As we look at our own faith in God, we will explore three distinct areas: faith is founded in trust and requires a willingness to trust; faith requires courage; and faith gives strength and energy.

Many people feel concerned about the status of their faith, wondering whether or not they have enough now and whether they will have enough tomorrow. They wonder exactly what it is and how to get it. We find ourselves looking to God to get us through the wilderness, but we don't know how much we need to depend on him and how much we need to depend on ourselves. Perhaps this continual personal search explains why so many of us struggle with the concept of faith itself—trying to analyze it, define it, and evaluate it. Unable to do exactly that, let us attempt to study something we can handle—faith that is based on a meaningful *relationship* with God. As our relationship pleases God, and as we pursue a constantly closer contact with God, our faith will grow.

What Is Faith?

You have enjoyed a Fourth of July parade at some time in your life, I am sure. You have seen the veterans and the bands; you have seen the flags waving and heard the speeches and shouting; you have felt a surge of patriotism rise in your breast. But that emotion is not true patriotism! True patriotism appears on the field of battle, in muddy, war-torn trenches stinking of death and destruction. Patriotism is found on the beaches when soldiers land and move forward to an unknown fate. Patriotism means the willingness to give one's life for the preservation of his country, family, and home. True patriotism exists not among the waving flags and cheering crowds, but in solitude.

Our Christian experience parallels this. Your faith is not found in the hearty singing of hymns from a pew on Sunday morning or in the fervent recitation of the Apostles' Creed. Real faith appears in your ability to face the crucibles of life. Meeting life's adversity—pain, suffering, sorrow—with calm acceptance: that is the experience of real belief. And we base that kind of faith on a real relationship with God.

Many people smile about faith because they claim it is naive. Perhaps this attitude is provoked by our unwillingness to live and act out our belief in our daily lives. We don't always practice faith in one another, faith in ourselves, or faith in God. We tend to believe certain things about certain people or certain aspects of life because it is the thing to do. We rarely make a real commitment to the simple things of life. And some of us fear that faith is a crutch. Well, it may be a crutch, but then we're all cripples who need just such support. Faith is a vital part of our lives and will become increasingly important as we exercise it.

Others say that faith is only applicable when the mind does not work any more. When you become intelligent enough, you don't need belief to explain any mysteries. Such people point out that you and I understand things that our parents and their parents could not fathom. We are a part of a society that is making strides in research at a constantly accelerating pace. How easy to fool ourselves into thinking that our faith becomes less and less necessary in direct proportion to our increasing intelligence.

But faith does not merely apply to things that are mysterious. Faith does, in fact, depend on the intellect to a degree. The intellect determines the foundation, the roots of faith, and therefore greatly influences your practice of it. You and I want to know about God. For example: Is God sovereign, or is he not? Does God know all things, or does he not? Is God everywhere present with the whole of his being or not? Is he the source of existence, or does he depend on someone else for life, like us? Is he mortal or immortal? Just what kind of a God do we have?

When Job's faith was being tested to the breaking point, God said to him, "Job, who am I? Who flung the stars into the heavens? Who created the great monsters of the deep? You know who I am, Job. Knowing me, why are you calling me into account? Trust me" (*see* Job 38–41).

I don't think Job's attitude is unfamiliar to you; it certainly isn't to me! For anyone who practices Christianity today, there is a tendency to call God into account. We demand this of him because we lack trust. And the same answer comes back to us that God gave to Job.

Knowing someone very well either builds a stronger faith in that person or destroys it. Thankfully, knowing our God better and better can only lead to a stronger faith. Our relationship with him goes back even further than our conscious desire to serve him—it goes back even beyond our birth. In Psalms 139:16 (NIV), the Bible says ". . . your eyes saw my unformed body. All the days ordained for me were written in your book before one of them came to be." God knew who we were going to be and cared for us even when we were in our mothers' wombs.

The mother-child relationship appropriately illustrates the relationship between God and us. Like a patient, long-suffering mother, God always loves us and gives us a solid basis for faith in him.

My own mother had enormous patience and commitment to me. I was a mischievous little boy. I know I tested the limits of her endurance regularly throughout my early years. She always seemed to understand me. When I was much older, she confessed that there were many times when she was sorely tempted to give up on me. But she was my mother, and she never forsook the belief that there was something good inside me. No matter how naughty I had been, no matter what trouble I got myself into, I knew I could go to my mother and find love, patience, and understanding. She cared for me.

When I had problems in school, I would rush home to my mother and pour out my heart. She always listened. There would be a word or two, here and there, as I told her about my concerns. I would unwind, and she smoothed things a bit and reassured me. Then with a lighter spirit, I rushed off to my studies or to play. I knew that someone far wiser than I had understood and helped me sort out my feelings. I shared a close relationship with my mother, an unbreakable bond. That relationship helped me understand what faith in God is all about.

In the midst of my conversations with my mother, there were moments of discipline and chastisement. In fact, I think that there were times when subconsciously I expected to be disciplined and in subtle ways let her know that I expected her to be angry. Yet as the years went by we remained friends. I recall doing things with mother and times of sharing projects or fun that were an important part of our love. We were bound together. The better I knew my mother, the stronger my faith in her became.

Not only do we have a personal relationship with God, on which we can base our faith, but we can also look at history itself. Unlike people of other religions, we can look back to times when God did certain things and find them documented in the Scriptures for us. We can study and ponder what has been recorded by historians; it is accurate. The Scriptures provide the foundation. We know that Jesus really lived; we know what he said, and we know what he did sufficiently well to be able to build a foundation for what we believe. But knowing all the facts is not faith; our faith is built upon these but requires more.

A Definition of Faith

What really is this thing we call faith? I believe our faith is composed of three basic elements. We must clearly understand

and acknowledge those if we seek true spirituality and a deeper
relationship with God:

Faith is *trust*—being willing to trust and believe.
Faith is *courage*—being willing not only to trust, but to take
action based on that trust.
Faith is the *energy* we need to take action based upon trust in
God.

We might return for a moment to the story of the orienteering course that opened this chapter. The two boys began the
activity with a basic friendship, but Matt had to go beyond that
to win the race. He trusted the judgment of his friend Jeff. He
had the courage to dig in and struggle when the going was
hard. His faith in his friend also gave him the energy to go beyond his own capabilities when Jeff led the way.

That analogy might hit close to the heart of anyone who has
ever seen life as a jungle or an uncharted wilderness. Faith in
God helps guide us through that jungle, but faith is a relationship with our Leader, not reliance upon our own abilities.

Faith Is Trust

The first basic element of faith is trust. We face many things
that are beyond our ability to understand or to deal with effec-
tively. Trust—knowing God loves us and wants the best for
us—is an enabling part of faith. God alone can give us the ability to really trust in ourselves, in others and in God's direction
for our life.

A little over two years ago, my wife and daughter and I were
at Mayo Clinic. The doctors told us that my wife could not live
much longer the way things were developing. As we drove to
Rochester, Minnesota, and enjoyed dinner together, we struggled to believe what these doctors were telling us. When we arrived at the hospital, for surgery, they invited us to review a
film on what to expect after surgery. How would the patient

look? What was all the equipment, surrounding the patient, there for?

I have gone in and out of hospitals for years. I have seen people in intensive care—scarcely living—but still breathing and with hearts still pumping because of the machines surrounding them. I thought I had seen it all. Then we watched the film. I must confess I had never seen anything like that. The next morning, the elevator carried my wife away into the hands of some men I had only met once before. Placing her life in their hands, she went into surgery—my daughter and I just watching and waiting, believing in what the doctors had told us. We believed in their medical skills enough to trust those surgeons and risk my wife's life. To trust in someone as we did at that moment is faith.

But in the case of our Christian faith, we don't trust God as we would a doctor. With doctors, the relationship begins in physical need and ends when healing has been accomplished. We don't expect God to heal us, make us better, just so we can get well and end the relationship. Our Christian faith remains. From our personal perspective, it may have a starting point, but it should not end. A doctor comes to us externally, but God comes to us internally. A physician cares for us until we are well, but God unites himself to us, never to leave.

Before we knew Christ, it was "I." Now it is "I in Christ." The old "I" diminishes as the new "I in Christ" comes alive. But it is no longer I who lives. It is Christ who lives in me, and the two of us are joined within. I trust him implicitly. I give him my life. Whatever he wants he may have. That is faith. That kind of faith goes on through the days of life and the days of eternity. Saying it is "I in Christ" requires trust.

An aged martyr named Polycarp said it all in the second century A.D. A furious ruler gave the old man a choice between denying Jesus and being killed in a hideous manner. Polycarp's trust in his Savior never wavered. He told the ruler that he would not deny a relationship that had been very real to him all his life. "For eighty-six years I have served him," Polycarp said. "He has never let me down. How can I deny my King who saved me?" Polycarp no doubt wondered why his Lord had led him through all those years and then presented to him a grisly death, but he never broke his grip on the hand of Jesus. He had shared life with Christ; he would also share death with him. Although he was burned at the stake eighteen centuries ago, Christians still remember that man's unshakable trust.

Did you ever have a dear friend in whom you believed and then someone told you some gossip about that friend? Your response was: "I will not believe it; I know my friend too well. She would not say such a thing; she would not do such a thing." You trust her. You trust God in much the same way when you have faith.

Another example of unqualified trust is found in the story of Abraham, in Genesis 22. God asked him to sacrifice his beloved son. When God spoke to Abraham and said, "Take that son—the fulfillment of promise—and sacrifice him," it made no sense at all. But Abraham, by faith, went out to Mount Moriah, where he was willing and ready to serve God in obedience, simply trusting, not knowing what the future would bring.

Jesus also showed an unqualified trust in his Father. He did so in the face of pressures we human beings cannot even imagine. Some of his statements from the final hours of his life, recorded in Luke 22 and Mark 15, show the tension he endured as he followed God's plan. "Father, if you are willing, take this cup from me . . ." (Luke 22:42 NIV). "My God, my God, why have you forsaken me?" (Mark 15:34 NIV). The reply of the people who were torturing him was no help. ". . . If you are the king of the Jews, save yourself" (Luke 23:37 NIV). Through this hellish pain, rejection, and anguish, Jesus retained his faith in his Father. His final words on the cross were, "Father, into your hands I commit my spirit" (Luke 23:46 NIV). He remained faithful to the end. Jesus is our example: we, too, need to build unwavering faith. When God says "Trust me," we need to be able to do so.

In *Guideposts* Adela Rogers St. Johns tells the story of her own faith. She said, "It was like a great rope, and I wondered whether it would be strong enough to hold me in a storm." Then the storm broke. Her young son, Bill, joined the Canadian Air Force and was flying missions between England and the Continent in 1943. One day, she received a telegram: "Regret to inform you that your son, Pilot Officer William St. Johns, was killed in action." She learned later that he had gotten his plane as far as the coast. Seven of his companions had parachuted to safety, but he went down with his craft and was killed. She said that when the news broke on her, she could do nothing but sit down in total exhaustion and sorrow; she could not pray. She does not know how long it was, but finally she began to reach out and say, "O God, what happened?"

Somehow, she felt God saying something to her. "All is well with your child." A peace came into her heart, and she went back to her family. "It is well with Bill," she told them. "We talk about him, we know he is living; he is there, we are here. We miss him, but God claimed him. Though we do not understand, we trust him." Faith in God, for her, was indeed like a rope that held firm through the howling winds and dark hours of the night.

Faith Is Courage

We must also learn that faith needs courage. Faith does not exist without courage. It takes courage to get married, to say that from this day forth, until I die, my life will be intertwined with another's. It requires courage to give yourself in service to something that is greater than you can see at the moment. It took courage for Abraham to move from the Ur of the Chaldees, his homeland, to a country he did not know anything about and to difficult circumstances.

Commitments always take courage. But that is what faith is all about. If you do not have any faith, you do not make those commitments. Nor do you make the leap into the blind, unknown future, regardless of who is there with you. You try to freeze your security.

Faith is a great, exhilarating adventure! Experience faith by making that move when God calls! My wife and I look back on one of the greatest things we ever did. We left all we had to start from scratch in Oak Brook, Illinois. At thirty-nine years of age, we abandoned the security of a church where we had served for thirteen and one-half years to begin a brand new church. We turned from our denominational home to the unknown future.

I think a golden hour for our church in Oak Brook was when it decided to build a church sanctuary three times too large for its congregation. If we repeated that same level of commitment today, it would demand a mortgage in excess of $40 million. Would the members have that kind of courage again? I would like to think so. That is the courage of faith. Faith compels us to do things because we know that God wants us to do them. That same faith so influences us that we dare not refuse to do what God asks us.

We follow God wherever he leads. On occasion, that requires an enormous amount of courage. If you have never had the courage it takes to act in faith, I invite you to pray for it. Nothing makes you understand faith better than doing something that seems impossible but that you know God wants you to do. If you hesitate today because you feel you know what you ought to do but are not sure of success, trust God and do it! You will never regret it. Following God's leading reaffirms and authenticates the fact that you really have the faith you need. How poor the life that has never enjoyed a courageous adventure with God.

Faith Gives Us Strength

The third element that we must learn about faith is that we receive the energy and the strength that we need to obey. There is a very peculiar thing about faith. Once you become involved in obedience, you seem to have the strength and the endurance you need. Luther and Calvin wrestled with this. They came to the conclusion that when Jesus said God is the author of faith, he meant more than that it is by the power of the Spirit that faith is born in a heart. He also meant it releases physical power in you to fulfill the demands of God, if you will believe in him. I saw a beautiful demonstration of this recently.

Several years ago a woman in my former congregation discovered she had cancer. She was the only source of guidance and support for her four children and believed that she still had work to do for those children and that she had a great deal to give them. Her brother-in-law was a doctor, and he gave her the best counsel he could, but he could only shake his head after looking at her reports. She would not live very long. The woman accepted what he said, but in faith she also trusted that God would provide the strength for her to do what was necessary for her family. A year passed. Then two years, three years, and four years. God kept her going for many years after the cancer was found.

Two weeks before she died, she met me in the church foyer after the evening service and, with a smile on her face, told me how good God was to her. She was the picture of walking death. The next day, she went to the hospital and never recovered. Today her children are in Maine in the care of a sister—their aunt whom they scarcely knew. That mother—through those long years—had amazing staying power and physical endurance. Her faith was undying.

Soon after her death we received a letter from her son, the oldest child. He had started to go to a youth group near his home in Maine. He wrote to say, "I am going to keep with it because Mom would want it that way. . . ." He knew what his mother wanted, but here is the most important thing: ". . . and most of all, I want it that way." He caught what his mother had, and he talks in his letter about the example he can set for the younger children. He continues, "Thanks for everything. Everyone has been so good to us through our bad times, especially the church. Love, in Christ." It is a beautiful letter, written by a young man reaching out to a community of believers that he came to love, exercising the simple faith he had seen so energize his mother in those last years. Faith of that type has no fear, born from a love for God and sustained by trust in him. God will provide for you as much as or more than he requires of you.

Reach for that kind of faith in your life. For all who seek him will find; to those who knock, it will be opened. Without faith, we cannot please God. Trust, for trust forms an essential part of your faith. Have courage, for you need courage to act in faith. Let faith give you what you need, for a life lived in faith allows God to respond to your trust and your courage by giving you strength and energy to accomplish what you have set out to do.

As you begin to act in faith, you will find God's love pouring out of your life in numerous ways. Let us now explore the impact of God's love on your pursuit of spiritual growth in your life.

Study Questions

1. The author says that faith is part of a growing relationship with God. How is this true? How can you help deepen your friendship with God?
2. What is faith? Name the three elements the author lists and tell why each is important in the journey into joy.
3. What have you done that gives evidence of great faith? Was it rewarding? If not, what was the deciding factor?
4. How can faith be strengthened?

8

Love: Practicing God's Motivation

... The love of God is shed abroad in our hearts by the Holy Spirit. ...
Romans 5:5

Some time ago I officiated at a beautiful wedding. The bride and groom, a handsome couple, were very much in love. They came from good families and held deep commitments to each other. I had no doubt that their love was genuine and God would bless their marriage. I was to say a few words that would be appropriate to the ceremony. A five-hour speech would not allow me to touch on all the varying experiences of persons who love. Philosophers have written volumes on the subject! The subject seems almost greater than our human capacity to understand.

Yet, through the ages, we have tried to comment on love. Something in us wants to understand the awesome power of love. As I pondered the wedding ceremony, it came to me that their glimpse of love was like looking through a knothole in a fence.

121

Peeking Through a Knothole

In a sense, our understanding of love is like a child peeking through a hole in a board fence. Imagine for a moment that you are a youngster anxious to see a circus parade pass by. Looking through your special knothole, you see the animals, marching bands, brightly colored wagons, calliope, clowns, and a host of fascinating circus characters. You see only a little at a time, but every sight that passes by on the street registers in your mind. You store away all the images of the extraordinary things that passed by and are down the street where you can no longer see them. You have no idea what is still to come. Anything is possible! Beyond the limited range of your knothole will be things that you couldn't imagine in your wildest flights of fancy.

J. Wallace Hamilton in *Who Goes There?* says that most of us view life like a young child with his face pressed to a hole in a fence. We see only the sights that fall within our very narrow range of sight. Perhaps you actually remember peeking through such a place in a fence; do you remember how tightly confined your world view became? You could only see that which was right in front of you on the other side of the fence.

But how does this metaphor drawn from a childhood experience relate to our understanding of God's love?

There is someone above you who looks over the fence. He sees that which has already been and what is to come. He knows about things not yet come to pass. That someone is God. He views the full perspective, unlimited by the parameters of a knothole. When the director of the parade of life is someone you trust and someone you know loves you, it gives a great sense of well-being and stability to your life. You can say to yourself, "I realize I am only getting a knothole's view of life, but God has the fence-top view. From his position, he can see the full length and breadth of life's parade. He knows where my small piece of fence sits along the parade route." What assurance and comfort come from that perspective.

Do you feel that sense of well-being in your life? Do you know God loves you and cares for you as he always has? Do you sense that God watches out for you from high atop the fence and knows a great deal about your parade? You must also sense God's desire to talk with you. Because of his warmth and friendship, something within you feels compelled to respond. God's power moves you intensely, like no other force, yet it seems elusive.

Try describing a power that can move nations and change the world. Is it based upon true commitment, dedication, and desire? Would you also venture that such world-changing strength results from true giving of one's whole self with every ounce of one's energy? Does it find its origin in God's intense love and friendship for you and for me? I believe that God's love unlocks an enormous power within each of us, providing motivation to truly change our lives and the lives of others around us. In Romans 5:5, we read: ". . . The love of God is shed abroad in our hearts by the Holy Spirit. . . ."

God's love is vital to our Christian faith. The picture of a child peering through a hole seems also apt in describing our limited understanding of the love of God. We get a small view of his love as it manifests itself in our own lives or the lives of those close to us. We try to grasp the greatness of that love from the small yet influential encounters we have. But, like the child at the knothole, we see only a part of the big picture. We know what has gone on before, but we cannot guess what still will come.

As shallow as our comprehension of it is, God's love provides the foundation for our faith in him. That love manifests itself in a host of ways all around us every day. I remember reading the book *A Walk Across America,* by Peter Jenkins. He started walking in New England. When he got to Washington, D.C., the editors of *National Geographic* gave him a camera and asked him to take pictures as he walked across our great land. Partway through the trip he paused to write about some of his experiences. One of his remarks caught my eye, because it had so much to say about the power of God's love in our lives.

Peter Jenkins writes, "You know, the thing that impressed me the most was the love that was shown to me. It did not come from those who were talking about welfare programs because they loved the poor and loved the needy. It did not come from the people who want to make love and do so publicly. It did not come from those who live in communes. You know who it came from? Just the average Mr. and Mrs. America, building their home with their children, and willing to reach down into a pot that is almost running dry for their own welfare, sharing what little they have. They extended love to me, and every one of them confessed that they were, first of all, Christians, followers of Jesus." Jenkins is writing about love in action, love that cares, love that comes from God's love in our hearts. It is powerful, and it is obvious. Jenkins found that power as he traveled across America on foot; it made a profound impression on him.

In forgotten hamlets and lonely farm homes, Jenkins found pieces of a tapestry. As the weeks rolled past, the pieces fit together, and he saw the fabric of God's love permeating his experience. God was at work everywhere, he concluded.

As you look through the Scriptures, you cannot read through the Old Testament and into the New Testament without sensing that same fabric of God's love. Its power is evident throughout the Bible. In a sense, the Bible is nothing but a record of the love of God in the hearts and lives of men and women. That love pursued his people down through history and finally became incarnate in Jesus Christ. God's love for humanity—his creation—motivated him to give us his very best. He so loved the world that he gave his only Son. Jesus said to his disciples, "By this all men will know that you are my disciples, if you have love for one another" (John 13:35 RSV). That was the hallmark—the distinguishing feature—of the followers of Jesus. They loved a world that ached with hatred, bitterness, and resentment. God's love can provide us with the same kind of motivation and power, if we let him in.

Is God in Your Life?

How does God break into our hearts? How do we search our inner lives to comprehend the presence of God? What do we find when we look inside ourselves? How do you know that God is in your life? We must ask these questions; they are the prerequisite to tapping God's love and the resulting motivation. God must be a part of your life for his love to be shed abroad in your heart.

Yet these questions baffle many of us. Even though God is a spirit, he does come into your life. How does it happen? Something comes from God to you and then flows from you, out to the world. That outpouring of his love from us to the world defines the Christian. The world understands God's love as it sees it in you and me and recognizes that his love sets you and me apart from mankind in general.

Have you ever stopped to think about what God has given us? He has provided us with his most precious gift: his love. This love is almost impossible for you and me to understand. He *pours* it into each of us. Christian thinkers occasionally use the analogy of the hand and the glove to describe Christ's indwelling love: We are all like well-crafted pieces of fabric, made in the image of God, but until he puts his own love inside us we cannot do anything. We could carry that analogy a step farther by saying that we are as unable to fully describe this infusion of divine love as a glove is able to contemplate the hand that fills it. We know a little about the shape and activity of God's love, but we can not fully comprehend it.

Measuring God's love reminds me of a story in Zechariah 2 of a young man about to measure the walls of the Holy City, Jerusalem. At the time the story was written, Jerusalem symbolized God's special love because the Jews remained in captivity in another country, and God had promised that they would be able to rebuild the Holy City and go back to their homeland.

The prophet writes that he saw ". . . a man with a measuring line . . ." who announced his intention to measure the new

Jerusalem—to find out how long and how wide it was. The story takes an unexpected turn when an angel tells the prophet that the young man will never be able to measure the new Jerusalem. "And I myself will be a wall of fire around it," the Lord said to the prophet, ". . . and I will be its glory within" (Zechariah 2:5 NIV). No human measurement could apply to God. Are we like the young man? Do we try to circumscribe God's love for us and in us and thereby do it an injustice?

What does it mean to understand God's love within us? We recognize the difficulty in measuring it. Yet we struggle with it because we want to know. We want to experience his love both externally and internally. We wonder whether we really have the presence of God within us, but we still say, "Yes, God is in me." That universal affirmation is one that everyone wants to experience.

I remember reading about an actress who was asked by some well-meaning people to go into a prison to talk with the men on death row. She said, "What can I tell them? Should I say that they have to live better lives or be thankful, when they are waiting to die?" The person who had asked her to visit responded, "No. All you tell them is . . . God loves you. That is the good news. That is the essence of it all. God is love. He who dwells in love dwells in God." Because the actress was a Christian, she knew and understood God's love in her own life. Those men on death row needed to hear about God's love; they also needed to see his love in action in order to comprehend its power. The actress could show them a glimpse of that.

Do You Hear That Quiet Whisper?

In an effort to comprehend God's love, let us direct our attention to something very personal. I do not want to talk about the Holy Spirit moving through society and changing things, but about that quiet whisper within your heart that says, "God loves you." I do not want to consider Jesus' dying on the cross for the sins of the world as though it were some commitment, a thesis, or even a Hollywood drama. I want to stand, with you, and look again at the cross and say, "Jesus died for me."

Do not just think of the Father as one who created the vast universe. Think of him as Paul did, writing in Ephesians 1:3, 4: "The God and father of us all knew us from before the foundations of the world." Jeremiah expressed it, "He knew me before I was born" (Jeremiah 1:5). God relates to us as we look within ourselves. There we find his love, which changes us by making us into new creatures. It totally transforms our attitude, for his love offers us a new vision of life.

God has always dealt with his people in love. It is the same love that has always been. See how he dealt with David in the depth of his misery (Psalm 30). Look at his response to Paul, who claimed to be the greatest of sinners (Romans 8). Consider the change in Saint Augustine, from an immoral man to one filled with God's love. Look how he transformed the life of Chuck Colson. Whether you view him historically or in the light of today, God remains the same. In spite of our limited ability to grasp his tremendous power and love, we recognize that he cares deeply for us. We know God's concern and compassion always existed—in history as well as today—and will continue with us for all eternity.

Accepting the fact that God's love remains a constant part of our spiritual walk is very important. Our lives hold a host of unknowns. We face new challenges and opportunities each day. What the future holds in store for our families, our jobs, our health, and more we can only guess. Understanding that God's love is a constant source of strength and a solid rock upon which to stand gives us a freedom to look ahead with expectation and anticipation. Great motivation results as we reflect on the knowledge that God's love will give us the power to overcome obstacles; his love will flow through us to others when we alone do not have the power to love. Tap into that energy in your life. God's love gives us the ability to see beyond the immediate, to raise our sights from knothole to fence top. I am reminded of how God's love enabled Joseph to accept his situation.

The story can be found in Genesis 37–50. Joseph was a special young man who dreamed dreams. He sensed that God had something in store for him. Unfortunately, when Joseph shared some of his dreams with his older brothers, they found his tales difficult to swallow. I think when he told them that someday they would bow down before him, Joseph's brothers had heard all they could stand. It was bad enough that their father had favored him with the coat of many colors. As you may recall, the brothers decided to sell Joseph into slavery and told their father that Joseph had been killed by a wild animal. I doubt Joseph had any idea what was happening the day he was sold as a slave to be taken to Egypt. A faithful child of God, Joseph had tried to serve him in all that he did. He was tuned into God's speaking in his life and tried to understand what it all meant. Now his brothers had sold him as a slave. For many years, Joseph never saw his family. His father did not even know that he was alive. His brothers only imagined his fate. Yet in spite of enormous adversity, Joseph held fast to his beliefs and trusted in God's constant love in his life.

Years later, Joseph's brothers became forced to travel to Egypt, looking for food during a lengthy famine. Joseph's dream as a young man was fulfilled. His brothers ended up bowing down to him, though they did not recognize Joseph. He said to them, "You meant it for evil; God meant it for good." He recognized that God had been with him through the years and that he had a purpose in all that transpired. Can you imagine the emotions that must have passed through Joseph when he saw his brothers kneeling before him and realized that all the plots and subplots of his life were reaching one grand climax? God's ends were accomplished. His presence was felt.

We Need to Affirm God's Love for Us

Not all of us live to see the events of our lives come to a single, dramatic climax, but as we march forward on the journey into joy we will begin to feel God working through us, accomplishing his will. God's presence becomes very real, and he affirms his love for us.

This ongoing affirmation is more than a pleasant benefit of

godliness: It answers a deep need inside each person for nearness to God. We draw closer to him as we see him using us to
accomplish his ends. This mark of spirituality meshes with
prayer, meditation, solitude, fasting, worship, and the reading
of Scriptures to produce great peace. We *know* God is present
in our lives. We can come to him without fear. We can seek,
knock, or ask because we know that we shall find. His love *is*
"shed abroad in our hearts."

God Understands Perversity

We experience this dynamic presence of God day in and day
out, in good times and bad. His presence in our lives during
times of tribulation is especially welcome. The bad times may
come about through external influences, or they may result
from our own internal shortcomings. Through it all, God remains. You probably know the adage that love is blind. God's
love is anything but blind. He knows everything and understands everything. Yet through it all, he loves us. He has an
unfaltering, unquestioning, unstinting love.

We humans cannot fully understand that kind of tough love.
Like me, you might have had occasions when someone you
loved dearly did something to kill your love. He pushed you to
the limit of what you could stand. When it happened, you
didn't see how you could ever continue to love that person.
You may have found yourself praying God would give you the
capacity to love him, because you could not call up love from
inside yourself. God understands that we have within us the
seeds of perversity. He stays with us. His love remains in us,
and it still overflows so others can see it.

One of the richest examples of such unqualified love is
found in the Old Testament story of Hosea and his wife,
Gomer. Gomer prostituted herself. She denied her family, her
husband, and everything to which she had committed herself.
She rejected love itself. But Hosea was a godly man. In a society that punished such behavior with death, he forgave
Gomer over and over. He pursued her unrelentingly. Hosea let

Gomer know that his love for her was without reservation, without concern for her behavior. Hosea finally did get his wife back; he had to buy her when she was auctioned as a slave, which was the accepted treatment of prostitutes in that time. When Gomer had nothing to give him, when she had insulted him and destroyed his reputation, when she had broken his heart, Hosea reached out in love to her. Knowing all about that woman's sins, he took her back to be his wife (Hosea 3).

God's forgiving love and unfailing concern are like that of Hosea for Gomer. While you and I may not identify with Gomer—a prostitute—our story reads very much the same. We know deep within ourselves that, no matter how badly we fail, we can come to God. No matter how miserably we fall short in our struggle to attain his high goals, God still loves us and accepts us. He cares unconditionally, even though he knows all about us. What a great assurance! Out of devotion to us, he gave his most precious love: his only Son.

God did it for you and me. Not in the abstract, but in a very real, tangible way. When you look inside yourself and feel that assurance of his love, you know that God is there. He loves you and strengthens you. His love is extended for you to receive it. That is his gift to each of us. Do you want to know if God is in your heart? First, look to see what he means to you and to your life. There are several clues that point toward God's presence.

God's Love Gives Us New Life

The first sign that God's love flows through you is this: You have been changed inside. You have been recreated. You are "... a new creature ..." (2 Corinthians 5:17).

An old Greek myth, the story of Pygmalion, carries none of the weight of Scripture but serves as an interesting reflection of this idea. Pygmalion was an artist who sculpted a statue of a beautiful woman. As the man gazed on the statue day after day, he fell in love with it. Yet it was only a statue. It could not see or feel or express emotions. Still Pygmalion loved the thing. His love grew so intense that it brought the statue to life. Pygmalion's deep love for the being he created gave her the ability to love in return. The myth contains a glimmer of the feelings we have as the creatures of God.

God made each of us. He gave us our unique qualities, our beauty, and our character. But until he infused his deep love in us, we, too, were like Pygmalion's statue. We could not begin to love each other until we first knew God's love for us. But his power and love are so great that we find true life in it. God's love surrounds us and makes us a part of his family. Without his love, we remain estranged and far off. We stay distant from an understanding of love and unable to comprehend love in its fullest, richest sense. Coming to know God's love, being filled with his love, teaches *us* how to love.

With his love we look at the world through new eyes. We are concerned—just as God is concerned—because we dwell in him and he dwells in us. The world becomes not just a place where our needs are met, but a spot where we can give to others who have needs and burdens. We reach them with love and concern because we have the resources of God's love within us. His love is our strength, and it can be the strength of anyone for whom our hearts ache. Because that love belongs to him, it is limitless! The more we give away, the more we will find within ourselves. It is a constant supply.

God's Love Is Not Ours Alone!

Another clue to knowing that God is in our hearts is a feeling that God's love is universal. His indwelling love spills out from our hearts. It crosses social and ethnic barriers, international boundaries, and cultural divisions.

Sometimes we encounter people who think they are among the blessed few to share close contact with God. Such people give the impression that God has some sort of heavenly pecking order. At the bottom are cave dwellers, and then probably Hottentots, then a little higher are Eskimos or Peruvian peasants, then perhaps Germans, next the British, and at the top are Americans. These smug individuals exhibit an attitude that seems to put these words in the mouth of God: "On the sixth day I created man, on the seventh day I rested, and then to cap it off, in 1776 I created Americans!" By their actions these narrow-minded individuals indicate that if more and more people would think like Americans, the world's problems would be solved.

I'm not like that, you may be thinking. But think again. In the dark corners of our minds remain feelings that certain people are beneath us. It might be a single person—perhaps someone who has hurt you. It might be people on skid row, whom you feel have squandered their God-given opportunities: The stinking, muddleheaded drunk sleeping in an alley seems not worth your concern.

A Boston preacher said, "I believe in the fatherhood of God, the brotherhood of man, and the neighborhood of Boston." Everything fell neatly into place in his hierarchy.

God does not parcel out his love according to neighborhood boundaries, city limits, or national borders. When his love is in us, we open our embrace to the world. Such love and concern are far different from the standard attitude of the human race. Their direct flow through us, from God to others around us, makes us unique. We become committed to those in need. We feel optimistic about the future.

Examples of world-embracing love can be found in many places, but Christian mission fields are full of intriguing stories. As you come to know real mission work and missionaries, you see the demise of the stereotype of the pith-helmeted, culturally insensitive religious do-gooder. The majority of Christian missionaries in this century have been dedicated men and women fueled by love. I have always found it interesting that medical personnel—doctors and nurses—work hand in hand with evangelists on most mission fields. They come from some of our best medical schools and often spend their lives in backwater towns in struggling countries. During the early years of this century, they also risked their health or their very lives by working in disease-infested parts of the world.

In South Holland, Illinois, a suburb of Chicago, there lives a ninety-year-old woman who was among the first Christian medical missionaries to work in the Persian Gulf area. Her work was hard, dangerous, hot, and lonely. Several of her co-workers and their children died on the mission field. Fanatical Muslims in the area had no use for the missionaries. But they persevered. Today, when you ask the woman what led her to such a difficult spot and kept her going there for forty years, she unhesitatingly says, "Love—a God-given love for the people."

At a low point in their history, the Children of Israel were forceably transplanted into a different culture, the Babylonian Empire. Psalm 137 recounts how they wept in the foreign land. Perhaps their pouting showed how low they had sunk spiritually. If they had felt God's love and had poured their hearts out in song, they might have had an impact on their oppressors. Joseph refused to bemoan his fate when he was a captive in a foreign land (Genesis 39), and Paul and Silas sang hymns when they were locked in prison (Acts 16). The Israelites in Babylon apparently had no love to share with anyone, while these other heroes of faith let God's love flow through them into the lives of others.

Why Love Is the Greatest Power

Love lasts. In time, the brick, mortar, and steel of buildings and churches will be gone. We see it throughout our cities. Ground once considered sacred and holy has now been abandoned by God's people. Churches are being torn down in big cities to make room for high-rise offices and hotels. But when the buildings are all gone, and you and I are gone, *love* will prevail.

You continue to live in the lives of those you have touched with love. Nothing remains quite so permanently as the love that flows through you to your family, friends, neighbors, and the hungry, the starving, and the lonely.

If ever our nation needed an expression of love, it is today. In these trying times of increasing numbers of unemployed workers and growing numbers of people who need to know that someone cares, you and I are called to respond with God's love. Look within your heart and ask yourself: *Am I really compelled to care? Can I resist giving to those in need?* Your answer will tell you if you have the reality of God in your life. It will show if God's love is shed abroad in your heart by the Holy Spirit. That love totally captivates and spreads naturally, even as God himself could not contain his love.

As you pursue a richer spiritual life and seek to walk more closely with God, do not overlook the tremendous resource at hand. God's enormous love is yours to draw upon and share. Once you are filled with his love, it quickly begins to overflow. You will find it pouring forth to your family, to your friends, to acquaintances, to strangers, and to those with needs around the world. Tap this resource and be filled with God's caring. God gave us his Son as a demonstration of his intense love for us. It was the thing he most valued above all else. When you pray to Jesus, be reminded of that. In Jesus' death we find eternal life; in Christ's dying we understand the unqualified, unending love of God. Let it be shed abroad in your heart by the Holy Spirit—today.

Study Questions

1. Relate the importance of our trusting God to his love for us. Can one work without the other? Why? How does this fit in with our study so far?
2. Consider some of the biblical stories that exemplify our relationship to God and his relationship to us. How do these help us understand the responsibilities and favors his love bestows upon us? Does God still act this way today? Give some examples.
3. What are some of the clues that show God is in our hearts? Have you experienced them in your life? How do you know? Can you help someone else experience these, too?
4. Do you love people? How do they know you love them?

9

Joy: Feeling What You Believe

Rejoice in the Lord always. . . .
Philippians 4:4 (RSV)

Some people always try to be "up." When you meet them on the street and ask how they are, they always respond, "Great!" "Fantastic!" or, "Never better!" When you get around to conversation, you find that their jobs have never been better, their families are supremely happy, and their children are all high achievers. Their spouses fulfill every one of their needs, their churches do incredible things in their community, and all their friends enjoy life to the maximum.

As things go from rosy to positively superlative, you begin to worry about the true state of affairs. You suspect your friend may be hiding something. You try to find a chink in the armor or a gap in the facade. Life couldn't be consistently joyous for anyone, you reason, and such whitewashed poppycock could only cover up something terrible!

We mistrust this kind of person. But when we read our Bibles, we find that joy is to be a constant part of every Chris-

135

tian's life. The Bible describes *continuous* joy, too, not just special moments of happiness. "Rejoice in the Lord always," we read in Philippians 4:4 (RSV). Does this mean Christians need to paste on happy faces and pretend that everything in their lives is happy? Weddings, births, job successes, and achievements are all fine—but what about ongoing, outpouring joy from deep in the soul? How can we discover true joy that comes from deep inside?

A few years ago, a member of my congregation named George was seriously ill with a rather rare disease known as myasthenia gravis. He remained in the hospital while doctors tried to find a treatment for the disease. As he lay in the bed, with tubes and wires coming out of almost every imaginable place on his body, he slipped in and out of consciousness. From time to time he would awaken fully and be able to converse with family and friends. During one of those brief spells of consciousness, his wife and I drove to the hospital to see him.

It happened to be George's birthday. In her hands, his wife, Louise, held a beautifully wrapped gift. *What,* I wondered, *could she buy for such a seriously ill man?* When she told me the box contained a gold wristwatch, I felt amazed! With her husband desperately close to death, time seeming to run out before it should, she gave him a timepiece as a token of her love.

When we arrived in George's room, Louise opened the box and removed the watch from its holder to show it to her husband. His eyes lit up with delight, and I recognized that this couple were looking beyond the immediate and ahead with anticipation and joy to the days when George would be better. After more than forty years of marriage, it never occurred to either of them to view the situation in anything less than its most positive light. Their joy, optimism, and enthusiasm for what lay ahead remained undeniable.

My mind flooded with a mixture of emotions, I felt that I nearly missed a profound lesson: For George and Louise, joy was a constant part of life, not just something for a special moment. They were even able to find joy in the midst of staggering adversity!

Joy in Adversity

True joy can and should be a part of our Christian experience, even when times are hard. When Jesus started his Sermon on the Mount, he first told his audience what it means to be *blessed* (meaning "happy" or "joyous"). As you read Philippians 4, you see a series of affirmations, and then Paul says, "Rejoice in the Lord always . . ." (RSV). The phrase leaps from the passage. Paul does not say, "Rejoice when things are going well," or, "Rejoice when God has answered your prayer or provided assistance in overcoming some burden." Paul says that we should rejoice constantly.

Do you sometimes think it difficult to be joyous? Do you feel the world pressing in around you? Do you weary from the demands of your family or your career—or both? It would not be a surprise if you read this passage of Scripture from Philippians and raised your eyebrows in disbelief. Joy is not a part of our society. Our generation is more attuned to the stress, the hardships, the strife, and the dismal side of life.

Only the things that are bad, not the things that are good, seem to make the news. As Christians, we become particularly burdened by what we hear because we feel compassion and concern for those around us. Whether people are our neighbors or are halfway around the world, we struggle with a desire to do something to help alleviate their suffering. Yet each night we listen to television announcers review the doom and gloom of the day.

The current approach to television news has prompted Jimmy Breslin to say that the news anchormen have the manner and appearance of well-bred undertakers, who night after night are portending doom for the world. We get caught up in what they say and wonder whether this is the time to be happy. What right do we, as concerned Christians, have to be filled with joy when so much trouble surrounds us?

For one thing, we have the teaching of Scripture. We cannot pick up our Bibles and begin to read without being impressed at the striking contrast we find therein. Joy is characteristic of the Christian. The New Testament is full of joy—the joy of individuals and of the church as a collective body. Just as joy became a vital part of the experience of the early church, it should be a part of our experience today! Worship ought to be one of our happiest experiences in the entire week. You and I ought to anticipate our worship that way.

Unfortunately that isn't the case. Our gloom-and-doom society affects the way we live out our faith. At some point, between the time of the early Christian church and the present, we have lost our joy. Through the years, happiness has lost its role as a primary part of our expression as Christians. I think you recognize this slow shift. The church concentrates its energies on the analysis of truth and the study of doctrine. In a sense, every clergyman becomes a dogmatician, looking at propositional truth and arranging it systematically in an effort to explain what Scripture has to say. He looks at ethical problems and makes judgments concerning right and wrong. This stance has earned ministers a place in our society that closely compares to judges or jurors; they have become rather sober individuals!

And there are times when we pastors are loud-voiced prophets of doom. The human heart is so full of wickedness that the best defense becomes a thundering offense. We shake our fists, we pound the lectern, and we rattle the rafters with our rage.

You may have heard about the young man who went to the airport to meet a minister who was to come and speak at his church. The young man did not know the man by sight and had to guess which was the pastor as passengers came away from the gate at the airport. Finally, the young man spotted someone who looked as if he must be the minister. The lad approached the passenger and said, "Excuse me, sir. I presume you are the reverend." The passenger replied, "No, it's my indigestion that makes me look this way." Is that the picture that you have of the clergy? Unfortunately, that image is too often the norm. We have somehow gotten the idea that such sobriety dignifies the office.

Whatever Happened to Christian Joy?

As we read the Scriptures, we see that the early Christians sensed the living presence of Jesus Christ. In First Peter we read about the joy of the believers. They were happy to be associated with Christ and his church. "Though you have not seen him [Jesus Christ], you love him; and ... you believe in him and are filled with an inexpressible and glorious joy," Peter says in 1 Peter 1:8 (NIV). Those new Christians could not contain themselves. Something gave them inner peace. They were joyous! People nearby could plainly see it. Those around them understood that in the midst of the troubles facing these Christians—and there were plenty of problems for them, as you well know—they had a deep sense of well-being that reflected itself over every inch of their countenances.

You and I do not see Jesus Christ. Yet we know Christ personally and have a relationship with him and to God, his Father. We, too, should share the joy that the early church experienced. Our Christian faith is indeed a vital, a genuine commitment. Let that show forth in your life! The great general Napoleon pondered the joy Jesus imparted to the early believers and penned the following thought: "An extraordinary power of influencing and commanding men has been given to Alexander, to Charlemagne, and to myself. But with us, our presence has been necessary—our eye, our voice, our hands— whereas Jesus Christ has influenced and commanded his subjects without bodily presence for eighteen hundred years."

Napoleon was right. Today, more than ever, millions of men and women would die for Jesus Christ. In some countries, they still do. Christ is very real to those who believe in him. He is not an abstraction to be analyzed. He is not a historic figure to be left in the past; he is contemporary. He rose and lives in our hearts. Christ compels us, commands us, to follow him with all our hearts and minds and souls. With great loyalty, we follow him and express his thoughts and his moods with joy. Of all the things Christ gave to us, his greatest bequest was his gift of joy. He said in John 15:9–11 (NIV), "As the Father has loved me, so have I loved you. . . . If you obey my commands, you will remain in my love. . . . I have told you this so that my joy may be in you and that your joy may be complete." The deep, rich joy we find in Christ is our source of satisfaction and inner peace. The scope of this happiness is as great as the overflowing love we considered in the previous chapter.

What Is True Joy?

Joy touches our lives in daily tasks. The surgeon feels the glow of accomplishment as he completes a lifesaving procedure. Intense happiness fills the mother who bathes her newborn child. Few things surpass the simple delight of a young child building a sand castle on the beach on a sunny summer day. As the young construction engineer stands and brushes sand from hands, legs, and feet and sets out to find mommy and daddy to show off his achievement, his face radiates pleasure.

We may talk about joy, we may feel it, but do we understand it? Perhaps we never realize that this much sought emotion requires satisfaction of the soul, not of the mind. Mental comprehension cannot bring fulfillment unless an inner peace dwells within. Neither can mere possession of physical objects or achievement of great things result in happiness.

Joy consists of being, not knowing or having. The warm glow of the heart at peace with the world, the freedom from guilt and shame, knowing that God has forgiven the causes of misery in our lives, these form the basis for true joy.

The joyous Christian experiences the liberty to serve others, knowing that he is accepted. This self-assurance rises from the knowledge that he is loved just as he is, because God's love fills him. He no longer feels like an alien, but rejoices in his freedom as a child of God.

An undercurrent, a foundation, makes him rejoice just in being who he is and knowing that all is well. This kind of feeling descended on a Samaritan village when the Gospel was preached and the whole village came to life (John 4). The people who gathered there heard something that made sense in a seemingly lost and frustrated world. Even there, two thousand years ago, the world seemed to be going nowhere in a great hurry. The villagers looked at their lives with frustration and dismay. What was the point? When they heard the good news of the Gospel, they responded from their hearts and souls. They found a purpose. Someone cared. Someone, far greater and wiser and more powerful than they, understood. God in heaven watched over them.

In the Old Testament we read about Nehemiah. In the midst of rebuilding Jerusalem, after the Jews were released from captivity, the Jews experienced a deep sense of joy. In spite of those who came to threaten the progress of rebuilding Jerusalem, in spite of those who tried to destroy what had been rebuilt, Nehemiah and his people were filled with happiness that gave them strength to go on with their building (Nehemiah 12:27).

New Testament stories also describe great joy. When Paul came to talk to the elders of Ephesus—as he traveled back to what he knew would be a contest with the Roman authorities—he talked of unspeakable joy (Ephesians 3). He knew it in spite of the beatings and rejection he had suffered. Something undergirded Paul and gave him peace within. What made his soul so strong? Certainly it was the knowledge that, in spite of everything going on in the world, there was a God in heaven. That God remains right here with us today, just as he was there with Paul. He created the earth; he thinks and plans; he actively takes part in our world. God is not far off at a distance. He is right here—right now. He directs the events and activities around us. We are not here by chance and things are not happening by chance. When you know and accept this, it makes a difference. Someone's hand guides your life. That someone cares.

The only hope for modern men and women paralyzed by the fear of a nuclear holocaust springs from this feeling of God's love. Polls seem to show that this fear grips more and more young people. Pippa sang, "God's in his heaven—All's right with the world!" but today's young people sing, "The bomb's on the horizon—All's wrong with the world." Our media systems reflected this distress and played upon it when the television program about a nuclear strike, *The Day After,* was shown in 1983. Non-Christians who don't succumb to dark pessimism must either duck the issue or adopt the devil-may-care attitude of the bomber pilot in the film, *Dr. Strangelove.* This wild-eyed pilot decided to make the most of his last moments by straddling an atomic bomb in his plane's bomb bay, letting out a bronco buster's yell, and then riding the bomb to his death.

When all around lose their heads, the Christian keeps his. He or she remains calm, assured, and even joyful. The nuclear bomb may be the most destructive force ever created on this planet, but the Christian knows it is completely under the control of the God who counts the hairs on our head or the sparrows on the housetops. He cares. He is guiding the future of the earth.

Although we would not call Mahatma Gandhi a great Christian, we can learn some lessons from his service to his fellowmen, even in the face of great tribulation. Gandhi claimed to believe that truth was stronger than destruction, errors, and the evil in this world. He lived out this premise. Giving up a promising legal career, he gave himself generously, even to the point of death, for those he served. An amazing power was generated by his activity and multitudes of Indians mobilized. Joyfully, they joined their leader in marches filled with danger and hardship. They looked to him as a father figure. Gandhi is just a fallible human example of the enormous concern that God has for each of us. God's love has a much greater capacity to elicit joyful response in Christians!

God Cared Enough to Intervene for You and Me

The basis for a Christian's joy is to know that he deals with the One who ultimately cared for all the world. God loved enough to become incarnate and live among us. He did not sit off in the distance and tell us how to do things. God sent his most precious gift: his Son. When you know God cares that much, you find a foundation upon which to rest your soul.

God's intervention was at great personal cost. Another human example of this deep spiritual truth is found in the story of Telemachus. During the years when Roman emperors staged bloody spectacles in the arena, Telemachus watched human beings, stripped of their dignity, fight to the death with each other and with wild animals. Finally he could stand it no longer. One afternoon he jumped onto the arena floor and rushed between two dueling gladiators, shouting, "In the name of God, stop!" He was cut to ribbons in a moment, but his impetuous act stuck in the minds of many Romans. He became the last man to die for the amusement of the crowds in Rome. Because Telemachus cared enough to take a stand regarding right and wrong, a bloodthirsty era came to an end.

God cares. He is willing to come to us, even when we find ourselves in the arena of life. He becomes one with us. "I have called you my friends," he tells us in John 15:15. You know there is a God who comes to us in our plight and now controls the way things are going. What tremendous self-assurance can come from knowing that God intervened for us! It gives us a perspective, as Christians, that directs our lives. We move ahead with confidence.

I am reminded of a story that will help you to understand what I mean by God instilling a self-assurance and confidence in our lives. Many years ago, a woman in my congregation felt that she ought to return to the work force. She had raised her family and done a good job as a mother. That phase of her life was drawing to a close, and her children had each made homes of their own. Yet as she surveyed the workplace, she did not have the particular skills that lend themselves to jumping easily back into business. She prayed long and hard for God's direction. As she waited for his answer, she felt led to investigate particular companies and learn a little about the way management related to the employees.

During that period, the woman developed the clear idea that she wanted to go to work for a company made up of good people who cared about their product, services, and internal relationships. Her closest friends had to agree that those ideals were noble, but they privately worried if her standards might be too high. Finally her search drew to a close. She selected Chicago Bridge and Iron, an Oak Brook, Illinois, company, as the firm that contained all the attributes on her list. She made an appointment to talk with the personnel director about a job.

When she arrived, she learned there were no openings. Yet the woman had the strong feeling that she had been led by God to this particular company. This was the one place she ought to be, she felt. She asked to speak with the vice-president of personnel and was shown into his office. He was intrigued with her tenacity in light of her lengthy absence from the corporate world. He thought that he would humor her and listen to her story, then send her on her way!

The woman told him about her search for a company that held the same basic ideals she held. She told him of her prayers that the right situation present itself to her. She told him of her conviction that Chicago Bridge and Iron was the place she was meant to be. She was so convincing that he found himself telling her about a need for the creation of a new position.

This new job, the vice-president explained, wouldn't be very glamorous. In a recent reorganization, the files of two departments had become hopelessly scrambled. If she were ready to accept a unique position full of headaches, she could go to work sorting out the files. The woman accepted the offer without a moment's hesitation. When it was all over and the vice-president was alone again, he shook his head in amazement at the way the woman had talked her way into his office and then convinced him that she could fill a position he hadn't even created until she entered his office.

What had prompted him to offer her the job? Why had she so easily convinced him that he needed her on his team? He had to admit it was her enthusiasm and her joy. It was infectious! She exuded the joy of Jesus Christ, and he found that he

could not resist it. Just a year or so ago, that same woman re-
tired, after a long and successful career. Her joy had carried
over into every aspect of her job. She had done so well that
promotion after promotion had come her way through the
years. A joy that found its roots in Jesus Christ led to an exu-
berant life of service!

The Key to Knowing Joy

When we think of Christ's time on earth, we think of his
hallmarks of an inner calm and joy. We would be remiss if we
did not also look at his deep inner peace even in death. He
gave his life for us, gladly, and demonstrated an unparalleled
joy. Just as he then rose from the grave to live among us, we
must let him lift our lives from the sadness and pain around us
and fill them with peace. He can make Easter out of every cal-
vary in your life.

Imagine how incredible Easter seemed to the early followers
of Christ. Jesus' crucifixion was an overwhelming reality. The
people cried for him to come down from the cross. They
shouted, "What are you doing on a cross, if you are the Son of
God?" Little did they understand what God had in mind. You
and I are no different. We often cannot understand what God
has in store for us. Yet we know God has something in mind,
and whatever it is, it will be good.

That knowledge is the very basis of our joy. Our joy also
rests upon our faith and hope. Faith—as we explored in chapter 7—takes into account that what has happened in the past
will happen again. We summon the evidence of history, and
then we move into the future with calmness and deliberation,
because what God has done he will do again. As we bring the
past into the present, by accepting God's sending his Son to die
for us, we affirm our future.

The hope upon which we base our joy comes from our acceptance of God's trustworthiness. God alone can promise that
which has never happened before in history. We summon the
future and bring it into the present. As we bow our heads to

pray, we say, "Heavenly Father, you sent your Son to die for me. He has, through his death and resurrection, not only re-turned to be with you, but come to be within me. He died for my sins, and I can count on your forgiveness because of his in-tercession. [This draws from our understanding of God's role in history and the recent past as well.] I know you are a con-stant part of my life, and I find strength and joy in that knowl-edge. [This acknowledges the present.] Father, as I look ahead to this day—or this week or this month—I need your help, your enabling power, your wisdom, and your love within me. [This looks to the future.] Be with me, I pray, as I travel down this uncharted path; guide me, Lord. . . ." And your prayer would continue on to review the events you plan as you look ahead. What tremendous perspective comes from having God's hand on your shoulder each day.

Ours is the assurance of an eternity yet to be. Based on the faith that recalls the past and a hope that summons the future, we live with joy, regardless of the circumstances that surround us. It becomes a building block in our personalities. It is the condition of the soul of the Christian. How could it be other-wise?

Joy Must Be Lived, Not Analyzed

We *experience* joy; we do not analyze it. But it happens to us as it happened to the prodigal son in Luke 15. He knew he could go home. He knew his father would accept him. So when he arrived, his father met him and embraced him before he even had time to offer humble repentance. We read that the family made merry; they were joyous; there was feasting; the son had returned.

If you have slipped away from a close walk with God and a personal relationship through Jesus Christ, his Son, you can come back! When you find God, there is much joy. As Jesus said, "When the bridegroom is with you, there is no mourning and weeping." But some of us act like the prodigal son's elder brother. We stay at home, but we really only perform our duties. We do everything according to the Scriptures. We struggle to be right and good, but without joy. There was something very wrong with the elder brother. It all came to the surface when the joy found in the redemption of the lost confronted him.

I would like to borrow an idea from a friend of mind, Neil Warren, who was until recently the dean of the School of Psychology at Fuller Theological Seminary. In talking about something called the "prayer of joy," Dr. Warren gives directions for experiencing a unique kind of prayer.

Let's follow Dr. Warren's step-by-step directions, and as we go along you will understand the feelings that flow to the surface as the exercise progresses. Start by finding a place to relax. Put your feet on the ground. Sit on a comfortable chair, with your hands in your lap. Nothing should encumber you or distract your attention.

Begin by tightening your fists and scrunching your toes. Tighten every muscle in your body, feel every nerve as you tighten as much as you can. Then, relax. Feel the strain release physically. Close your eyes to the world and do it again. Feel the release of all that is pent up within you. Release the tension from your life. Then, sit back and relax in the privacy of your own quiet place.

Keeping your eyes shut, picture yourself in a beautiful place, perhaps deep in the woods or in the solitude of the country. Or imagine the beach along the shore of a beautiful body of water. See yourself early in the morning when you are out for a walk, perhaps with your bare feet just touching the water's edge. It feels good. You are alone, and the whole world is some other place. The sun rises, and no one is in sight.

Visualize the sun just starting to show as you look off into the morning mist. Suddenly in the distance you see someone coming toward you. You realize, as the person reaches you, that it is Jesus. You have just recognized him. He looks at you and says, "Good morning," and calls you by name. Then he assures you that he knows you, understands you, and loves you. He cares about you and your life.

Jesus goes on to assure you that the big questions for you and your life have already been answered. The circumstances through which you are going are well known to him. His Father is in control just as he was when Jesus walked the earth. Then as he leaves you, going on down the beach, you turn and wave to him. He waves back to you and is gone. Then it strikes you—that was Jesus! You see yourself cavorting down the beach because you have just met the Lord. He has reaffirmed to you all the things you knew all the time.

Your day is immeasurably brighter. Such a prayer reaffirms that God cares and loves you. Though you go through the valley of death, you will fear no evil, for he is with you. You do not always rejoice and praise him for the troubles you have, but you do so in spite of it all. You respond this way because, in your heart, you are at peace. The experience of joy affirms your love, your commitment to God. You can learn from this: Spirituality leads us ever closer to God when we rejoice in the Lord always.

Joy forms a vital part of your Christian experience. Peaks of immense joy are not unique to the Christian or the non-Christian. What sets you and me apart from the rest of the world is the constant joy that manifests itself in our lives, day after day. Finding that and tapping its great power will add richness and fullness to your life. Make Christ your role model and guide. The joy he showed in life and in death was a constant outpouring of the joy of walking with God. You can know that same feeling if you "rejoice in the Lord *always.*"

Study Questions

1. Do you find it hard to believe that someone can be "up" all the time? What is the difference between that attitude and one of real Christian joy?
2. Why did the early church seem to have so much joy? Can we have it today? What keeps us from having it?
3. Describe real joy and the things that help it grow in the Christian's life. Consider this in relationship to God's love for you.
4. Are you a joyous person? How can you help others develop a disposition of joy?

Part IV

Journey Into Divine Power

10

Healing: Accepting God's Powerful Touch

. . . Your faith hath made you whole. Go in peace. You are freed from your suffering.
Mark 5:34

A few years ago, I attended a Kathryn Kuhlman meeting in Pittsburgh, Pennsylvania. Following that faith-healing gathering, we returned to our hotel for a bite of lunch. At the adjacent table sat a group of students from Northwestern University. The students were sociology majors who had traveled from Chicago to Pittsburgh to study the phenomenon of healing. As I chatted with them I discovered they were not religious, and the spiritual dimension of faith healing meant nothing to them. Yet when I asked what they thought of the Kuhlman meeting, one student admitted thoughtfully, "I cannot deny that God was there at that meeting."

The student's remark was a profound commentary on the healing process. Even unbelievers sense the presence of God when healing takes place. A number of years ago an acid-tongued radio program host named Joe Pyne carried a

151

talk show that was heard throughout the country. He called himself an agnostic, and he delighted in verbally demolishing guests who claimed to have special powers or supernatural experiences. Once or twice a week he sparred with someone who had a particular religious message, and usually he cut the message bearer to ribbons with cold, scientific logic.

Even Joe Pyne, however, admitted that faith healing was a real phenomenon. It took a personal investigation at the Shrine of Lourdes to convince him, but he was honest enough to admit that something beyond his understanding was going on.

Almost everyone, at some point in time, senses the presence of God when a healing takes place. Some feel it in spectacular ways. There are reliable accounts of persons experiencing healing accompanied by a rush of divine power. Sometimes the burst of energy knocks them down.

Others feel it in quiet ways. A woman lay at death's door in a hospital in Sioux City, Iowa, a few years ago. While doctors and family members watched helplessly, an unexplained disease was killing her by inches. As her life hung by a thread, friends in her hometown began calling one another on the telephone and quietly uniting in prayer. The prayer chain was assembled at about ten o'clock at night. The next day the woman's husband drove back to their town and saw a couple of the friends.

"How is she?" they asked.

"Stabilized," the haggard husband said. "Last night the disease seemed to come to a halt. The doctors think she may start a slow recovery now."

The friends hesitated for a moment, then asked, "What time? When did things stabilize?"

Not knowing about the prayer chain, the husband thought back to the darkened hospital room and the hum of bedside machines. He estimated the time at which he first realized that the mysterious disease was arrested. A chill went down the backs of the friends as he said, "About ten o'clock."

Other people feel healing in slow, small ways. A persistent problem responds slowly to some kind of new treatment. A handicap diminishes, and therapy or medication slowly takes effect.

But no matter what kind of recovery process takes place, God is there.

When the subject of healing comes up, thoughtful people will recognize God's hand. But let's alter the subject a bit to emphasize the "scientific" aspects of healing. What would happen if you asked a cross section of people, at random, for the name of the person who most influenced the field of *medicine?* (People in our scientific age usually put medicine entirely into the realm of science.) I suspect that a popular response would be Hippocrates. Some people might think of Louis Pasteur. A few might point to the development of the polio vaccine under the leadership of Dr. Jonas Salk. Would anyone mention Jesus? Probably not.

I would like to submit, however, that the man from Nazareth is the one who most powerfully influenced the practice of medicine. Jesus cared for the sick, instilled in his followers a respect for the human body, and fostered a deep commitment and enjoyment in the healing arts. He himself used extraordinary means to heal the sick, but he created in his followers an appreciation for ministering to the sick in many other ways as well. Think of the Christians around the world who have dedicated their lives to healing others. Countless hospitals, outpatient treatment centers, health programs, leprosy settlements, and childbirth facilities have started through the efforts of Christian medical personnel who understood that God was able to touch and heal through them.

"If I Can Just Touch His Garment . . ."

You may recall a powerful New Testament story about healing. Found in Mark 5, the story describes a woman who had been ill for twelve years. While we do not know specifically what afflicted her, we do know that she had been to doctors, and they could do nothing for her. She exhausted all avenues of healing available to her. So she resigned herself to living in misery and loneliness, struggling to have as rich a life as she could in spite of her serious handicap.

One day, the woman heard Jesus was coming to her village. From the story, we do not know how much she knew about Jesus. But we know she firmly believed he had the power to heal her. He alone could rid her of her handicap. With great optimism, the woman went to see him.

Joining the masses of people about the master, she touched his garment surreptitiously. Jesus beckoned to the woman to step out of the crowd. He wanted to know who she was. And I think he wanted her to declare herself publicly, so that others might know of her healing. She needed to understand that in that instant a deep relationship had been born. He showed her that the act of healing her body resulted from her trust and faith. She could not go about her business and return to her daily activities without recognizing that her recovery had come from the miracle of her attitude toward him. Jesus wanted the whole person to be healed: body, emotions, and soul.

We are so much like that woman. When we have serious problems, we expect to engage in heroic efforts to solve them. We seek out the best specialists, expensive medicines, or treatment in faraway hospitals. We may pray about the situation, but in the back of our minds we feel that the ultimate responsibility for effecting a cure lies in our own pursuit of treatment. People who have no religious background sometimes take literally the advice of Dylan Thomas and they "rage against the dying of the light." Desperately, they travel to Tijuana for wonder drugs or avant garde treatments.

Finally, when all the options have been exhausted, the Christian realizes in his heart that God can provide true healing power, not just the strength to carry on the search. Then he turns to him.

Why do we need to wait that long? No matter what stage an illness is in, Christ's healing power is freely given. Think about the New Testament story we just explored. The woman had merely to touch the hem of Christ's garment to receive his power. His touch was just that easy to obtain.

I believe Jesus expects us to seek him just as he expected the woman in the story to come to him. He isn't a fireman who comes roaring in at the last minute to douse an out-of-control blaze. He isn't a mechanic who swings into action when the engine needs a major overhaul. He's a friend who wants to hear about our needs, because we have a close relationship with him. He wants to know about the backache, the sore joints, or the digestive problems. He cares. He experienced some of the same problems himself, when he worked long hours in the carpenter shop.

Our faith in our friend Jesus Christ enables us to draw on his healing power. We undergird that faith with prayer, meditation, solitude, and the other marks of spirituality we have been discussing in this book.

We Should Seek Healing, Not Magic

Healing should be part of the total relationship that we enjoy with God, not a last resort. It should result from our continuing close contact with Jesus Christ and the bond of trust that grows with faith. As Morton Kelsey says in *Healing and Christianity,* "Tragically, the church tends to make magic of the normative element of healing." Really we ought not seek magic. We should come to Jesus for more than just a physical healing. I think that is the point that Christ made in his conversation with the woman he healed that day.

Jesus welcomed her just as he does you and me. Come to him with your illness or problem; he expects you to. But recognize that he did not heal all the people of his day, just as he does not heal all the people of our day. In his wisdom, he sometimes chooses to let a particular disease or infirmity run its course. I'll have more to say about that later on.

Recognize, too, that when Jesus does see fit to heal, he can make the healing complete and total. As I reread the passage in Mark 5, I find it interesting that the woman's illness was incurable by the standards of her day. This is true in each of the healings he performed during his ministry. He accomplished the cures swiftly and easily, and he never had a failure. This provides tremendous comfort to the Christian who has to deal with an "incurable" disease. If Christ chooses to heal, he is able to do so. If healing does not take place, it is by his choice, not because he has insufficient power.

When we ask Jesus for healing, we are coming to the Great Physician. He has cured his people all over the world for centuries, always focusing it in the church. In the book of Acts we find three distinct healings, each of which gives us insight into the process.

The third chapter of Acts describes Peter healing the lame beggar. Calling upon Christ's power, Peter helped the lame man to his feet, and his ankles and feet were immediately strengthened. The people who saw what had happened amazedly stared at Peter and John. Peter made it clear to them that God's power caused the miracle.

In Acts 5 we find that Peter was held in high regard for the healings. The word spread to the extent that people would bring the sick to wait along the route that Peter was to take in the hope that he would pause to heal along the way. Peter did heal a large number of people by calling upon God's power to work through him.

The eighth chapter of Acts tells of Philip healing a number of the sick. Again he did so by calling on God's healing power to work on those who were afflicted.

Acts 14 describes Paul healing a crippled man. We cannot read the book of Acts without being touched by the faith of the apostles as they called repeatedly upon God's healing power. As you and I find times in our lives when we seek healing, let us turn to God with an awareness that his enormous power awaits our call. Let us call upon Christ to let that healing flow freely through us to others, if that is needed.

Jesus Heals More Than the Body

As we explore Christ's healing power, let us not lose sight of his ability to heal more than our physical ills. His strength had, in some mysterious way, been transferred to that woman in the crowd. She had laid hold of a great energy source that was transmitted into something physical on her behalf. But recognize that Jesus had a reason for healing more than the physical afflictions. He touched her emotions and soul as well, because he wanted to demonstrate the power of a relationship to God. God was within Christ as he healed that woman. Although he came to earth and took the form of a man, Jesus remained in direct contact with God. He called on God just as we should do. But he made it clear that the relationship must exist for restoration to take place. We must begin by correcting our alienation, our broken relationship, and then we can heal the body. Jesus was not on earth just to perform miracles. He was on earth to help us make the connection between healing and our relationship to God through him.

Today, as you pray, meditate, and spend time in solitude, think through your relationship to God through Christ. Work to understand God's purpose in your life. Try to clearly understand that relationship and work to make it grow. Your open channel of communication with God is important for healing and for every aspect of your spirituality. Tap into God's rich resources and power for your life. If you find it difficult to comprehend, then consider the passage in John 10:37, 38: "If I do not do the works of my father, do not believe me; but if I do them, though you do not believe me, believe the works, that you may know and understand that the father is in me, and I in the father." Christ is trying to help us understand the relationship he had, so that we might pursue one ourselves. That provides the basis for a total renewal in our lives.

We Need Holistic Healing

Today, medical doctors, therapists, and pastors all work together in the healing process. One person or one skill alone is not enough. A relationship exists between each of the contributing individuals that makes the total process work. One acting independently of another would not begin to accomplish what all individuals together can do. I think physicians have no idea of the impact they make upon a patient when they enter a sickroom. The warmth and compassion and healing they give, apart from medicine, affects the condition of the patient. The relationship between physician and patient is a primary contributing factor to the amount of healing that is achieved with the prescribed course of action.

A respected physician recently told me that he looks forward to the next twenty years of research. He believes that during this time research will explore the impact of the spiritual side of healing upon the physical recovery of the patient. While we all understand that the two are related, we are not too sure how they work.

We recognize that when a man or woman is right with God and, thereby, right with others, that person has every resource available to recover and to permit the body to recover from whatever disease may attack. Health is looked upon as the composite well-being of the *whole* person, not simply the physical person.

Jesus Is Truly Our Great Physician

As far as we know, in Mark 5, only the woman who reached out and touched Christ's robe was healed. Her cure in body and soul required that she identify herself and step out of the crowd. That must have been difficult for her. She had suffered for many years with a disease that put her in the position of a leper. According to Leviticus 15, any woman who had a discharge of blood for many days was regarded as "unclean," and people were to avoid contacting her or anything she touched. If anyone so much as touched a bench upon which she sat, he or she was directed to wash, change clothes, and stay away from others until the evening.

The woman had to avoid other people. When she came to Jesus and joined the large throng gathered there, she did everything she had been told *not* to do. She took the chance that others would not remember her, so she could enter the crowd and touch the Lord himself. She knew very well that by physical contact she would contaminate him. She must have felt his power come into her body and the cleansing take place. She sensed that, by touching him, she had transferred her contamination from herself to Jesus.

We need Jesus' cleansing power just as much as the woman did. What a comfort to know that when we come to Jesus for healing we, too, transfer our sins and diseases to him. In turn, we receive his purifying energy. You can see why the woman resisted coming to him after she had been healed. She believed he could heal her, but she doubted that he cared for her. In fact, the story says that she was afraid.

Did she fear he would be angry with her? Would he be outraged at the audacity of a sick woman who dared to come and contaminate him—the great miracle worker—with throngs of people following him? How would he deal with her presumptuousness? She came and fell at his feet in total fear, confessing everything. Then we learn the good news. Christ cares for those who come to him seeking cleansing. In fact, he told his disciples that he recognized the need of those who approached him for healing. Who are the people who seek healing? Those who realize they are ill.

Jesus Wants to Heal Us

The healed woman discovered what you and I need to understand. No matter how lowly we are, how insignificant our deeds, or even what we think of ourselves, we can come to Jesus with our burdens. He wants them. He will take those burdens from us with joy and give, in exchange, his restoration. Sometimes this is difficult to understand.

When I was a very young preacher, I heard and then met E. Stanley Jones here in Chicago. I had always admired him. He was a great man who—to a very ripe old age—maintained an excellent physical condition, with a very strong, robust soul. He traveled all over the Orient to preach the Gospel.

That day, at the luncheon, he told us how he had been called as a young man to go east to preach the Gospel. He was all excited about the calling of God. He left for the Orient, but partway there he became ill. His health became such a burden that he had to return to the United States. During a very slow recovery, he became resentful and angry. The angrier he got, the more his weakness seemed to overpower him.

Then one day he caught himself. He decided he had better surrender the situation to Jesus. He simply turned it over to Christ, saying, "Lord you can have my soul, and you can also have this malfunctioning old body of mine. It is all yours. I will do whatever you want, within the capacities you give me." Then he totally relaxed. All the bitterness and hatred drained out of his system. His body began to function as it should. He became a strong and vigorous young man. He lived to a ripe old age.

You may know the story of Catherine Marshall and her bout with tuberculosis. She finally came to a point of simply relaxing and giving her life to the Lord. In a chapter of her book *Beyond Our Selves,* entitled "The Prayer of Relinquishment," she describes how she turned to God on a September morning and cried, "I'm tired of asking. I'm beaten, finished. God, you decide what you want for me for the rest of my life." She tells how the tears flowed, how her expectations were at a standstill, and how empty her faith became. At this turning point of her life she received the healing touch of God.

The experiences of E. Stanley Jones and Catherine Marshall were like that of the woman who touched Christ in the crowd. When the woman was healed, Christ told her that her faith had made her whole. Then he told her to go in peace and quietness. She felt a new inner strength. She was freed from her suffering.

You can experience healing by accepting God's powerful touch in your life. It is not enough to simply place yourself in the hands of physicians and hope for the best. When you are ill, draw upon the strength you find in prayer and meditation. The skills of a physician and the power of prayer complement each other in the restoration of well-being and physical health. Your relationship with God is a vital part of the process.

If you were not concerned about your relationship with God, you would not be reading a book like this one. You are striving, each day, to grow closer to God in your daily life. You want to deepen the bond that you feel through Christ. This desire and your efforts to achieve a richer more meaningful relationship with Jesus Christ form an essential part of the healing process.

The Healthiest Way to Live

Faith overcomes all things. You have strength within your body to ward off what might defeat someone else. The healthiest life-style is to live in peace with God and fellowman. When Jesus came to give us healing, he came to extend it to the whole person. We will still suffer; we will still die. This is still a sinful world. Sickness is *not* a sin, but it is an evil. It comes upon us as a result of being here.

I touched upon the idea that Jesus does not heal everyone physically. He did not do so while he was here on earth, and he does not do so today. We must accept this. But if we walk more closely with him, he will guide us through our burden of sickness or hurt. He will do what needs to be done. You will recall that Job went through terrible pain and suffering in life. He found his strength, during the worst, by calling on God's power to ease the burden. He knew that the suffering was his to endure. Had God chosen to remove it, he would have done so. But God did give Job the internal resources to get through the experience.

When Paul was afflicted with the thorn in his body, he turned to God for healing. God did not cure Paul physically, but gave him the spiritual and emotional health to endure the infirmity. Paul said, of that experience, "Your grace is sufficient for me" (2 Corinthians 12:9). But when we come to God for his help, we must come with the right attitude. Our perspective should be that God alone can decide whether or not to remove the physical pain, suffering, or illness from us. If we must endure it, then we call on God to lighten our burden along the way. We ask God to give us the strength and wisdom to deal with the problem.

Three Important Points About Healing

Let's consider healing and the spirit. First, all healing is divine. It is a gift from God. Can you imagine what life would be like if disease could not be overcome?

Second, every doctor—whether or not he knows it—acts as an agent of God's healing power. How blessed the person is who reaches out to be touched physically with both the medical knowledge and the restoration that he has experienced within his soul. We take what the doctor does and combine it with our habits of faith, bringing together health and healing under Christ.

Finally, remember that the practices of spirituality are the most healing forces there are in all the world, for they make us whole. They bring harmony in our lives, enable us to overcome troubling character flaws, and lead us to restore broken relationships. Through them we may forgive and forget those incidents or words that may have lurked in our minds, causing resentment and bitterness. Our memories and our emotions can be repaired. They thereby provide the body with the optimum conditions for physical health.

What this world needs to see is what that crowd with Christ needed to see—followers of Jesus coming out from oblivion and anonymity and making themselves known. Our generation needs Christians who are willing to tell all who will listen what it is that makes them healthy and enables them to endure suffering.

Try a Daily Dose of Psalm 103

An acquaintance of mine has for many years suffered with a very serious illness that includes both weakness and a handicap that makes each day a difficult undertaking from beginning to end. This friend told me that each day she begins with Psalm 103. She said, "Before I even get out of bed in the morning I spend a few minutes in prayer and then recite the first verses of Psalm 103: 'Bless the Lord, O my soul: and all that is within me, bless his holy name . . . Who forgiveth all mine iniquities; who healeth all my diseases; Who redeemeth my life from destruction; who crowneth me with lovingkindness and tender mercies.' "

Ponder these words for a moment. It brings together all of what we have considered in this chapter. Your sins are gone in Christ. Because of your relationship to Christ, you find power and strength that you would not otherwise have within you. Your health is secure because you are in constant contact with the one who cures. His love will flow through you as a continuous source of healing if you let it. And if you do not receive physical restoration, you have the assurance that you will find the spiritual and emotional recovery that you require.

May you find Christ's source of strength in your life and healing in Christ's words to the woman who touched the hem of his garment: "Go in peace; your faith has made you whole. You are freed from your suffering."

Study Questions

1. The author says that wherever a healing takes place, God's hand has been at work. Do you agree? Why or why not?

2. What would it have been like to be the woman described in Mark 5 before, during, and after the healing? How do you think she felt? Do you think she understood what was happening?

3. What are some of the mistaken attitudes people have about healing? Discuss them in light of what you have learned here.

4. Why was it important for Jesus to heal the woman in body, mind, and spirit? Consider the effect this kind of healing could have on people today. How could the medical profession benefit from Jesus' methods?

5. Does everyone need to be healed? What kinds of healing are there?

11

Worship: Experiencing the Divine Presence

... Hear the word of the Lord, all ye of Judah, that enter in at these gates to worship the Lord.
Jeremiah 7:2 (KJV)

A number of years ago, the entire group with whom I was traveling waited with great anticipation for word that we might have an audience with Pope John XXIII. Finally word came that we would have the opportunity to go before this great man of God who was the catalyst for so much change in the Roman Catholic Church.

We talked at length the night before we were to meet the pope, conjecturing on what would happen. The next morning, we awoke very early in order to make sure that we were properly ready for the exciting day before us. I remember taking extra care as I shaved and dressed, to be sure that I looked my very best. All the while, one thought was on my mind: I was going to see Pope John XXIII. I could think of nothing else during breakfast. The time seemed to drag as I joined the others in my group to wait. We were all conscious of the tremendous influence this man had around the world.

At last the time came, and we were ushered into the Vatican. It was every bit as exciting as I had imagined. In the midst of unbelievable splendor and majesty sat a man dressed in magnificent robes. Yet as I approached him I felt struck by the humble kindness radiating from his eyes to each of us gathered there. He seemed unaware of his great power as head of the Roman Catholic Church. There was no doubt that he was a man of God.

I could not help glancing around at others in my group to see their reactions to the experience. For some this was a sort of worship. It seemed as if they were before God himself as they stood in complete awe. Others approached it reverently, very conscious of seeing an individual who personified the church for millions of people around the world. For some, it was simply one of life's high points. Each of us found it a moving experience.

As we walked out of the great rooms of the Vatican into the bright afternoon sunshine, I reflected on what I had seen. I am not a Roman Catholic, so I suppose I have been a bit more objective than some of my Catholic friends. Yet I still found myself thinking how much anticipation and expectation had preceded our meeting with the pope. I found myself almost ashamed that I could expend so much nervous energy for an audience with another human being, when I often took an audience with God himself for granted.

In a very real sense, you see, time spent in worship every Sunday morning is an audience with God. How do you prepare for it? Do you take extra care to ready yourself? Do you pause to reflect on who you are and what a great privilege it is to come before the throne of God? Do you look forward to paying homage to your Creator?

Since my audience with Pope John, I have approached worship with much more care and preparation. Pope John may have been a great man, but God is so much greater that there is no comparison. Time spent in worship is time spent experiencing the divine presence.

Taking a Look at Worship

Throughout the ages, men have assembled for worship. The Old Testament is full of accounts of people worshiping God. In the New Testament, Paul tells us that we must present our bodies a living sacrifice, which is our ". . . spiritual worship" (Romans 12:1 NIV). Our worship today is much different from that of the Old Testament or even that of the New Testament. In the early days, people did not come before God directly. Within the temple a great curtain divided the people from the Holy of Holies. Only the priests were allowed into the innermost room that contained the Ark of the Covenant and the law. And even the high priests only appeared before God there once a year. At that time they sprinkled blood on the Ark of the Covenant. That blood represented the death of sin and was symbolic to the people of that age. It meant God would forgive the people for their sins because they believed, they prayed, and they sacrificed to him. But the people could not come before God directly. They had to accept what the priests said. A great curtain separated them from God.

When Jesus died, the veil was destroyed, and the Holy of Holies was opened to men and women of the temple.

Because Jesus came and took the form of a man, people in the early church were given the ability to contact God directly. They heard him speak, they saw his miracles, they saw him die, and they touched him after he arose from the grave. When he ascended, they understood that he would somehow come back to be with them. He told them, "I will always be with you. Where two or three are gathered, I will be there" (Matthew 18:20).

These early Christians must have had a mix of feelings when they gathered in the upper room on Pentecost. About 120 believers were there when the Holy Spirit came. God came right down among them, with the sound of a torrent of wind and a display of flames of fire above their heads (Acts 2:2, 3).

Worship, for these people who were touched by God, became a rich experience. How well they understood, in the following weeks, that God was truly in their gatherings of two or three or more! These were not mere customary rituals (as too many modern worship services have become), but vibrant meetings to honor Christ, listen to him, love him, feel his love, and know him more deeply.

Can you and I have equally rich worship experiences? We know the same living Christ. He welcomes us to come to him. No invitation is needed. We can worship him anytime and anywhere. Unlike people who seek an audience with the pope, we do not need permission to visit God. We have a seeking, pursuing God who calls to us. We are his people. God welcomes us as we gather in church to worship him. He receives us over and over—as often as we gather in his name. Because of his awesome ability to be everywhere present in his entirety, God does not require us to set appointments or fit into a schedule. In contrast to the formal petition for a brief moment or two in the presence of the pope, our time with God is limitless and freely given. We have the joy of knowing that when we gather to meet him he *will* be among us.

People who don't know God or understand worship often criticize the service. Like armchair quarterbacks, they come up with all kinds of analyses. They fall into particular categories: the free-form advocates, the do-your-own-thing advocates, and the *ad hominem* people.

The free-form people snipe at the structured aspect of most worship services. They proclaim that true fellowship with God would be free of convention, unfettered by standard procedures, and free of prearranged order. What they don't understand is that the discipline of assembling in a particular place on a particular day is good for human beings whose lives have a tendency to become slightly disorganized. By following particular patterns of worship, a person can focus on God and not on unexpected variations in the experience. God honors gatherings convened in his name; and by scheduling gatherings regularly, worshipers are exposed to God regularly.

Even though a service may be structured, we never know what will happen when we expose ourselves to God. One thing we can be sure of, in fact, is the unpredictability of the Holy Spirit. The meeting may be the catalyst for making changes in our attitudes and activities. It may give us unexpected insights and show us things within ourselves that we never before recognized. Within each service are the seeds of change.

A second kind of critic is the do-your-own-thing advocate. He wonders why Christians need to come together. Why not take a walk through the forest and commune with God all by yourself? Isn't solitude something like worship, as long as a person draws close to God? We answer these critics by emphasizing the value of face-to-face contact with fellow believers. In our culture, we are much too quick to seal ourselves off from one another in our automobiles, in the little space between our heads and our television sets, or in the protective tent of an open newspaper. Christians cannot practice their faith in a vacuum. We need one another.

Other critics of the worship experience zero in on "hypocrites" in the pews. When they see a few weaknesses and foibles in the people in church, they write off the whole practice of worship. In response to their criticism, I can say that Christian worship is unique. Church is the only place in the world where people gather with their families, loved ones, friends, and acquaintances to say, "I am a sinner. I need forgiveness."

The confession of faith that is a part of the worship service is a special blessing. Those who feel dirty in their souls and in need of cleansing make that admission and then receive the assurance of God's blessing. Like so many other parts of worship, this is an essential ingredient in the reconciliation of God and his sinful people.

We can't come to an understanding of the richness of true worship by analyzing the critics, however. Let's take a positive look at worship.

Direct Contact With God—The First Dimension of Worship

As Richard Foster said, we gather to ignite our spirits with divine fire. We crave this because we so love God and because he loves us in return. God cares about you and me, and he wants to be with each of us. In turn we come expecting his presence in worship. The first dimension of worship is our direct contact with God.

That direct contact is totally unique. Nothing else measures up to it or has the same purpose. Our meeting is with the God who created all things, who fashioned the heavens, and who created microscopic things. God created the minute cells and even more minute chromosomes that make up our beings. He blesses us with all virtue and goodness. When we know other people who are good, it is because God is good and has blessed them. As we come to meet him, we come to the source of all that is good and powerful and wise and eternal. He is God. The church is the place where we meet him each week. For that kind of meeting, we should prepare ourselves carefully.

Community—The Second Dimension of Worship

Next we consider the people side of worship, which we call community. Worship is entirely different from being alone with God. We explored being alone in the chapter on solitude. Now we are examining the part of our time with God that is spent collectively with our fellow Christians. Worship means the corporate experience of meeting God. The Holy Spirit unleashes mysterious power when God's people come together. Public worship is the scriptural way to release that power. Things happen to a congregation of God's people that never could happen to an audience of attendees at a program or a group of students in a classroom. Indications of such blessings are found in the Old Testament tabernacle and temple worship as well as in the New Testament church services. No substitute exists for the corporate worship experience. It requires a great deal more than analyzing law and precept or virtue and more than performing a mental exercise or trying to understand something.

Why Do People Worship?

What inside a person needs the worship experience? Why do Christians worship? In the seventh chapter of Jeremiah, we read about the Israelites' difficulties in this area. A good king named Josiah had previously instituted a number of religious reforms, and at that time the Israelites had begun to return to the kind of worship that their God-fearing fathers had practiced. Then Josiah died, and the people had the responsibility of continuing his reforms themselves. They continued to keep the Sabbath day, but they started slipping into many immoral practices during the week. Jeremiah writes about the flagrant transgressions of God's law in chapter 7: thievery, murder, adultery, perjury, fraud, covetousness, and treachery. Everything in the nation was deteriorating, although Josiah had established reforms.

Why is this passage appropriate to our examination? It contains two important elements. First, while the Israelites were obviously committing very serious sins, we must be mindful of our own faults during the week. You think, *I have never murdered, or coveted, or stolen! What is the point of comparing me to the Israelites of Jeremiah's time?* Remember that we often commit sins of the heart and mind. Have you ever resented someone else for his material possessions? Have you ever wanted something so badly that you could not get it off your mind? Have you ever had such unkind thoughts about someone that you later felt ashamed? These shortcomings form an obstacle to a close relationship with God.

Prayer, meditation, and solitude help restore our relationship with God. A right relationship through Jesus Christ is important to our worship of God the Father. Be reminded as you think of the concerns that Jeremiah expressed in Chapter 7 that our sins cannot be ignored. Jeremiah tells the people that they must hear the word of the Lord as they enter to worship. He urges them to refocus their thoughts every week. Worship requires that we regularly set aside the concerns and burdens of the week and really center our attention on God.

The second element in the passage from Jeremiah is that worship had become meaningless to the Israelites. Filled with liturgies, it was a formal process overflowing with propriety but lacking emotion. Worship relieved some guilt, salved their consciences a bit, but did not change anything. Returning to their daily lives, they never gave the Sabbath experience another thought. Jeremiah makes it clear that the worship of the Israelites left God out. He urged the people to meet with the Lord, because he knew that he would speak to them. If they truly listened, they would find him. The people needed a re-birth of genuine worship wherein they would come to meet God and feel his presence.

Jeremiah understood the importance of feeling God's pres-ence in worship. Once they truly sensed his presence they would not return to the sins and transgressions of their daily lives. Because of their contact with God the Israelites would not continue to go against God's law and feel right about it; it would increasingly bother them. Finally, they would find themselves on their knees in prayer, asking God's forgiveness. That is what worship is all about. Nothing in the world equals it.

Do you sense the connection between the Israelites and yourself? Jeremiah speaks to you and to me as well. When he says, "You who enter these gates to worship the Lord, hear the word of the Lord," he makes a powerful statement. As we gather we must hear the word of God.

Jesus spoke about worship many times in the New Testa-ment. One particular passage in John 4 provides insight into what Jeremiah was saying in the Old Testament. In John we read that we should "worship the Father in spirit and in truth, for such people the Father seeks to be his worshipers." Jere-miah said it; Christ said it; we must get beyond the form and function. Understanding God's truth alone is not enough. We must also be filled with his Spirit. The Spirit and truth together enrich our worship.

As you prepare for the service, try to arrange your schedule so you arrive in the sanctuary a few minutes before the service begins. Use the quiet moments to contemplate God's truth re-vealed in Scripture. Open yourself up to the Holy Spirit. Be filled with the Spirit. Be filled with God. I firmly believe that our Sunday-morning worship experience is just a small taste of what we will experience when we gather with the great throngs who live in God's presence. People of all ages, races, and colors will gather together to praise God and bless his holy name. Let us work to make our Sunday gathering as much like that as we possibly can.

Why Do You Worship?

We have explored why the Israelites worshiped in the Old Testament and how Christ views the role of worship in our lives as believers. What does it mean today? Some people consider worship one of a number of options open to them. They believe that it is not necessary to attend church to be a Christian. Others make comparisons in their minds. For these people, attending church is just like attending Sunday school. And so they make a choice; they attend church or Sunday school as if the two performed interchangeable functions. Other people feel that worship is simply an adult exercise, not a place for young people or children. Some think of it as a sort of "religious program" including singing, praying, and an inspiring speech. A variety of elements make up the program—like any other program—except that it is religious in tone and quality.

Did you find yourself nodding your head and saying, "That is exactly right; that is what worship means to me"? Did you find yourself saying, "No, that isn't quite right. Worship is more than that to me"? In either case, I hope you will examine why you go to church. I worry sometimes that there are those individuals who go primarily to meet friends or to refurbish their social life. Worship, for them, is a tangent to their real reason for being there. But let us explore the ideal approach to this subject.

What Worship Can Be for You

Worship holds great potential for the Christian. It provides a time to gather with other Christians to praise God. We draw close to God. During this very personal time, we allow God to touch our hearts and renew our spirits. We have an audience with God. Earlier in this chapter I mentioned my audience with Pope John and my careful preparation for the meeting. Ever since then I have tried to be more careful about preparing for my audience with God on Sunday. I am not talking about just showering and dressing, although that is somewhat important; I am most concerned about preparing the heart and mind for this experience.

Let me share with you some personal reflections and tell you a bit about my own church, Christ Church of Oak Brook. Each Sunday we gather in a place that has been especially built to help us to worship. Christ Church was designed to point heavenward. Inside the sanctuary, the beams were left uncovered. The resulting architecture reinforces the visual power that moves our eyes naturally upward toward the central bell tower. The building materials are strong, simple, and plain, with quiet, restful colors. Within its walls one feels serenity. The sanctuary shuts out the world, and the light of heaven shines down from the heights on all who gather there.

As the congregation enters the sanctuary, they pass under a massive cross that seems to float above the door. After worship, the cross is the last image that people see as they leave. It serves as a humbling reminder of God's presence there. Our church is a dedicated, holy place. The structure has been set aside for one purpose only: It is God's special place to meet us. People have told me that it does something to them to be there. They gather in the sanctuary, with anticipation and expectation. Worshipers often bow their heads in prayer when they first arrive, asking God to be there with them and looking with conviction for results.

Each week, as Saturday draws to a close, begin to prepare for the morrow. Make your Sunday-morning worship special. As you awake, pray for the experience that is ahead. As you dress, hold thoughts of anticipation for the service of worship. Even as you drive to church, focus your thoughts on Jesus. When you enter the parking lot at church, pray for those you see around you. As you walk toward the church, intercede for those you meet and who greet you. If everyone gathering in a church were to do this as he approached the church itself, it would create a mutual exchange of concern and prayer. As you sit in your pew, readying yourself for worship, lift up to God those who move into the pew next to you and persons you see coming down the aisle and taking their seats. No one knows what burdens their hearts.

Few families are without hurts, and Christ Church of Oak Brook contains many families. I often become aware of the enormous amount of pain and hurt within my congregation. Those persons need the prayers of others as they come to church. They come with burning needs. More than anything else, they need prayer that God will indeed meet them there. I am sure that this is true in your congregation as well. More than anything else, pray that the people you see around you in worship will be different for having been there. Ask that their burden or concern will be lifted. Bask in the knowledge that others are praying for your unknown concerns at the same time. By the time the choir and pastor arrive, you will feel a certain electric, spiritual dynamic at work. I know that this is true at Christ Church. We feel that something will happen, and it does.

Through the years of my pastorate, I have seen many people arrive at our worship services with obvious feelings of eager anticipation. Because they came to church with the expectation that something would happen, it did. They waited to meet the living Christ, risen from the dead, and they did. They waited for God's Spirit to fill them, and he did. The renewed spirit they hoped for they found there.

That same spirit of expectation filled the Christians of the New Testament. Though they had no Bible, the early Christians' rich oral tradition told them about Jesus. They learned what Jesus did and what he taught by passing the stories along from one to another. For them, worship meant gathering to hear someone tell them about their living, risen Lord, who was present in their world. All but one of the apostles were martyred because they believed that Jesus was alive, risen from the grave. When they met for worship, they met to be with him. They did not gather just to discuss his deity or to analyze one of his parables. They came to have him touch them because he really lived among his people. Their worship was a personal, intimate, collective contact with God, through his Son, Jesus Christ. We long for that same kind of contact today. I have seen it happen and I continue to see it happen. Let me share the stories of several individuals.

Anything Can Happen if . . .

First, a fellow we'll call Mr. A. came to a worship service with a blunted conscience and absolutely no intention of doing anything about it. Over the years he had become adept at justifying dishonesty. He padded expense accounts and mixed personal business with time he was supposed to be spending on company business. Then he started cheating on his taxes. It wasn't a big step for him to progress to marital infidelity. All along the way, he managed to justify his behavior in his mind. He attended church now and then, but it was only for appearance' sake. He made no effort to truly worship God or even listen to a sermon.

Then quite unexpectedly, the words of one sermon cut into his mind like a sword. The morning's topic was personal integrity and accountability before God. The layers of justification the man had created to shield himself from admitting his own faults fell away.

Although people around Mr. A. couldn't see what was happening to him, he went through several emotional upheavals as the sermon progressed. He felt a crushing burden of guilt and shame. He prayed silently for forgiveness. An inner peace so intense that he almost broke down in tears flowed through him. He knew the Lord had forgiven the mountain of guilt that he had felt so strongly. By the end of that same worship service, he felt cleansed and challenged to live a life of service to the Christ he had met in such a powerful way. Although I suspect that the man may not have followed every subpoint in my sermon, I know he entered the sanctuary as a callous, minor-league sinner and left as a new man. Since then he has made amends with his employer, he has completely altered his attitude toward paying taxes, and he has begun making up for lost ground in his family relationships. Mr. A. now is an active church member, and he is beginning to see new dimensions in his religious life.

A teenager's life was altered as he tried to sneak into a worship service. His parents insisted that he attend services, so he put in appearances just to keep peace in the family.

On this particular Sunday, the young man slipped into the last row as the minister was praying. He slouched down in the pew, intending to ignore everything for a half hour and then get on with more interesting pursuits. But God had other plans. A sentence in the prayer seemed to leap from the pulpit and burn into the youth's mind: "Lord, send dedicated people to labor in your vineyard."

The young man never could get that statement out of his mind. It became a clear message to him—*he* was to become a laborer in God's vineyard. He went on to college, seminary, and then to a richly blessed careeer as a minister of the Gospel.

A young woman came to our church service one morning. She was rootless, mixed up, and totally immersed in the secular philosophies floating around her college campus. She dreaded the future and wondered if her own life would be worth living. The fear of nuclear holocaust clouded her mind. War, strife, and bitterness were all she could see in her future.

In a Sunday-morning worship service she caught a vision of the mighty God who through all generations has been Lord. In a deeply emotional experience, she met the God who was able to take even the injustice of the crucifixion and fashion it into a great blessing for all mankind. Suddenly she saw hope for the future. Never again would the philosophers of gloom and doom rob her of zest for life.

The music in the worship service is much more than "filler." At Christ Church we integrate the music with the spoken word, and we also strive to present special numbers that will be a blessing in themselves. A woman I'll call Mrs. B. came up to me after a service that included some songs from Handel's *Messiah*. With tears in her eyes, she gripped my hand and asked me to thank the musicians for bringing her closer to God.

Some people are more sensitive to a ministry in music than others, but everyone understands the thrill that can touch a person's heart during a rendition of the "Hallelujah Chorus."

Then there was Mrs. C, an older woman who for many years had been a widow; her life was filled with boredom and monotony. Nobody seemed to care about her.

She attended church regularly, but on one particular Sunday a passage of Scripture spoke to her as never before. It was a message based on a text she had heard preached many times over the years: "Come unto me, be yoked with me; let me pull the heaviest side of your load for you" (Matthew 11:29, 30). The woman felt God touching her. She *felt* God was telling her he cared and he was there beside her all the time.

Like the others, Mrs. C. had a deeply satisfying experience as she sat quietly in the church that Sunday morning. People around her probably didn't realize what an impact the service was having on her—but then again, there were probably others who were experiencing their own spiritual reactions to that same service.

On many occasions, I have had someone quote back to me an obscure phrase—months later—that I did not even remember. The Holy Spirit took that phrase and burned it into that person's heart. The phrase became the needed focus for change. If you come to meet God in worship, anything can happen.

I have something I would like you to try in the coming weeks and months. It is a tool for preparing for Sunday worship and a habit I hope you will keep as long as you live. Visualize yourself in God's presence. If you are at home, see yourself at church. Think of the presence of God surrounding and filling you. Picture yourself sitting in the pew and praying for others just as they pray for you. Imagine the expectation that you feel as you anticipate what is yet to come. Then see Jesus coming into the sanctuary. In a very real, living way he has come to bless and to heal and to renew your life. Envisage the joy you feel as you realize that you are in the presence of almighty God. He welcomes you and makes you feel you belong there with him as he smiles radiantly. That smile tells you how meaningful and important you are to him. In his eyes you see forgiveness and understanding. His look tells you he wants you to share your burdens and concerns with him. He seems almost eager to lift the heavier side of the yoke you carry. You are aware that he is God; you stand in awe of him, and yet you recognize that he was willing to become a human being and to suffer even death for your sins. You praise him and worship him for the many things he has done in your life. You acknowledge his vast power and his still, quiet presence in your life. God is right there with you.

This technique of visualizing the worship experience in preparation for Sunday will help you ready your heart and mind. Spend some time in preparation. Worship means drawing near to God. Scripture tells us he will draw near to us in return.

I hope you see that worship is an important aspect of your journey into joy. It alone, just like prayer or fasting, is not enough. You will find great power, renewal, and growth if you bring together all these ingredients in your life. Take time to pray, to meditate, to be alone. Fill your life with joy, and love. Act in faith. Make worship the capstone of each week. Make it the high point and the culmination of all that you aspire to be and to do as a Christian. Open your heart and let God touch your life.

Study Questions

1. How does worship differ from the other aspects of the journey into joy that have been presented here? Why is it important in the Christian's life?
2. Critics of worship use many tactics. Name the three that the author discusses and describe them. Have you ever been tempted to believe them? What effect will their attitudes have on the Christian's walk with God?
3. Why is it important to spend some time preparing for worship? Is this something you do regularly? If not, how can you establish the practice in your life?
4. Does worship have spiritual significance for children and young people? How will regular attendance affect their adult years?
5. What elements of worship help you focus on God's presence?

12

Balance: Joining the Heart and the Mind

. . . God chose you to be saved through the sanctifying work of the Spirit and through belief in the truth.
2 Thessalonians 2:13 (NIV)

In a distant land there once lived twin brothers, Thinker and Feeler. Thinker was a fine, dutiful man, respected by all. His brother Feeler was an equally upright man, much admired for his piety and pure heart.

One day a man named Evangelist passed through the land, bearing an urgent and troubling message: "Flee from the wrath to come." The twin brothers listened attentively to Evangelist. Thinker asked many questions and was deeply moved by the precise, well-considered answers. Feeler listened attentively and felt an urgent need to respond to the man's warning.

"Show us where to go!" the brothers said.

Evangelist pointed to a road in the distance. The brothers could see that it led toward the Slough of Despond, Vanity Fair, the Valley of the Shadow, and rugged mountains. "You must go on that road to Celestial City," Evangelist said.

"We go!" the brothers announced. Leaving their homes, families, and friends, they embarked on their journey.

After they had struggled through the Slough of Despond, a curious thing became evident. Neither brother walked on the center part of the narrow road to Celestial City. Thinker trudged on one edge and Feeler marched on the other. Sharp stones, ditches, dense brush, trees, cliffs, and other hazards lined the edges of the road and impeded their progress.

"Come over to my edge of the road, brother," Thinker would say, as he picked his way through bramble bushes and roadside boulders. "I have catalogued all the twists and turns, and I have important insights that will speed us toward the Celestial City!"

"I cannot leave this edge of the road," Feeler would reply. "I feel in my heart that I am getting closer and closer to Celestial City, and I would be foolish to change sides now!"

Even as he spoke, Feeler stumbled over an old log and bruised his knee.

"You are in error, brother," Thinker said. "I fear you are deluded when you say your edge of the road is the best. I tell you that I have a much better understanding of things than you. Why, I will even have a map before long!"

"You are mistaken," Feeler shouted. The brothers separated as they walked at different paces, and they had to shout to make themselves heard. "Insights are not enough. Inspiration and the simple joy of the journey are much more important!" Feeler called.

Thinker didn't reply for several moments as he waded through a flooded ditch. "No, brother, you are wrong, wrong, wrong!" he then shouted. But Feeler was out of earshot and did not hear.

That was the last communication between the brothers for several weeks.

They had separate adventures and encountered a variety of friends and enemies on their journey. Some foes lurked on one side of the road, some on the other, while still others waylaid travelers on either side. Thinker seemed to have the most difficulties with obstacles that were not recorded on his maps. Feeler occasionally blundered into barriers because of his occasional practice of shutting his eyes and pushing blindly ahead.

After three or four weeks Thinker and Feeler came together at a freshwater well. Bruised and tired, they stretched out and tried to regather lost strength. After some minutes, they began to converse. They talked about the journey and shared experiences. Thinker showed Feeler some of his maps.

"I do not possess maps like yours," Feeler said, "but I have learned some lessons about the best manner of making progress on the narrow road. In certain kinds of conditions, I felt as if my feet had wings."

Thinker pondered his twin brother's statement, then gazed back at the road on which they had come to the well. In his mind, a thought hatched.

"Can you indeed teach me what you have learned?" he asked.

"Yes, brother."

"If I were to use my maps and your counsel, I could be greatly assisted on the journey," Thinker mused.

"I might benefit from you, also," his brother said.

From that day on, Thinker sought out the advice of his brother. The two traveled together from time to time, and when they faced great difficulties they marched together as one person. As the weeks passed, Thinker took new joy in the pilgrimage. When his maps were insufficient, he relied on the lessons he learned from his brother.

Something unexpected happened when Thinker began crossing over to the other edge of the road. He spent more and more time walking on the center part of the road, and for the first time he realized that the journey to Celestial City did not need to be a constant struggle against obstacles that spilled onto the edges of the path. He often raised his voice in song as he marched along.

Feeler, too, walked closer to the center of the path as he used his brother's maps. No longer did he move ahead with eyes closed, but clearly saw the hindrances ahead. He faced them with his brother, as they helped each other over large rocks that barred the way. Together the twins took the shortest route to the Celestial City. As Feeler sang the refrain of his brother's tune, life seemed full and wonderful.

A Matter of Balance

The story of the pilgrims summarizes much of what I have been trying to say in this book. We Christians often make our spiritual journey much more difficult by limiting our approach to either analytical understanding of God's way or to emotional heart commitment. As I indicated earlier, I traveled for many years on the cerebral, academic side. I believe that Christian brothers and sisters who stay exclusively on one side of the path do not realize how much they limit their Christian life. Certain that theirs is the only side, they don't even consider other options.

If I had to summarize these thoughts in a single sentence, it would be this: "Spirituality is not only an intellectual endeavor; it is a matter of the heart."

If I were to highlight one particular word, it would be *balance.*

Spiritual growth comes when you take the things you know and allow your heart to work with them. Growth occurs when you balance an analysis of Scripture for its form and content with an appreciation of Scripture for the way it speaks to the heart.

Balancing the analytical with the emotional is a little like setting the delicate mechanism inside a fine pocket watch. We might also think of the old-fashioned scales once used by chemists. We strive for perfect balance, but at the same time we know that there always will be room for improvement. The Christian welcomes the opportunity to draw closer to God. The fact that this process will never be complete in this life need not discourage him. In fact, it might be *dis*couraging if knowledge of God were so shallow that we could plumb its depths with little effort!

The Benefits of Balance

Could you benefit from the balance we are discussing? Look over the following questions. Answer yes or no to each.

1. Do you feel a need to strengthen your relationship with God?
2. Is your prayer life exciting and satisfying?
3. Do you pray often?
4. Do you take the time to listen to God? Do you know how?
5. Do you regularly break away from the rush of daily activities and commune with God?
6. Do you feel that God is near you and concerned about you?
7. Do you feel good about yourself? Is your self-esteem high?
8. Is your life well focused and "simple"?
9. Are you able to discipline your body to help you focus on spiritual things?
10. Do you truly believe (without fear) that God cares for you?
11. Does love fill your life and spill over to others around you?
12. Do you really enjoy living the Christian life?
13. Do you feel God's presence as you struggle with sickness or infirmities?
14. Do you feel God's presence in the worship service in your church?
15. Do you feel a need for "something more" in your spiritual life?

You probably saw the direction the questions were taking as you read through the above list. If you answered the first and last questions with a yes, and many of the other questions with a no, then you are indicating a need to touch God. If you have been walking on the analytical edge of the Christian path, then you need to balance your life with a closer relationship with God.

I know it is possible to be a committed Christian and still not feel close to God. For that reason, I hope you are not reading this book just to gain an *understanding* of the journey into joy. If you came to this book just for intellectual stimulation, you may, in fact, be disappointed. The things I have discussed are all recorded in other sources, and you may already have studied many of the topics.

I want you to *feel* deeply about each of the topics, to struggle for God's blessing just as Jacob struggled with God (Genesis 32). I want you to share the richness of life in Christ, and after that I hope you will pray, meditate, fast, believe, worship, and pursue all the other disciplines mentioned in this book. Use your mind and your emotions—together.

Are you able to recognize that God has the power to heal and has performed miracles throughout history? That's not enough! Such understanding cannot even be compared with falling on your knees and receiving his healing touch. Have you gained a renewed appreciation for fasting as a method of drawing near to God? That's not enough! You need to *feel* the ache of the stomach and the cathartic hurt of a system without food for many hours. Analyzing the beautiful experience we call worship is not enough. Go to your church next Sunday and experience God in the pew beside you. I hope your faith is tested in coming weeks. I hope it grows. I hope a friend or acquaintance stops in his tracks next week and thinks, *What's going on inside that person? He's positively radiant!*

I hope you have hurts, joys, problems, and challenges that will help you *feel* the presence of Christ in your life.

The difference between *understanding* the concepts in this book and *feeling* them is something like the difference between analyzing and experiencing love. Research papers have been written about the biological aspects of male-female relationships. Whole sections of bookstores are devoted to the topic. A student of such things could read day and night for years and not cover all the material that is available. Even hard-line behaviorists who have no respect for romance are forced to analyze the thing we call love. We dissect the topic endlessly.

Then think about the young couple in love. Do they care about all the books written on the topic? Do they stop to analyze what is happening to them? They only know they are experiencing something powerful and beautiful. It affects what we call "the heart." Light years of distance lie between the analytical books on love and the feelings these two share!

Love for a child is the same kind of experience. I remember my daughter and son-in-law before the birth of their first child. They read books on parenting, they attended classes on how to care for the newborn, and they read magazine articles. But the moment that the doctor placed their newborn son in their anxious arms, a flood of comprehension swept over them. They felt the maternal and paternal instinct. The little baby was theirs. They were forever bonded to the child. The experience took a new shape when their hearts felt what their heads had known all along!

Our spirituality is like that. It becomes real when our hearts feel what our analytical minds have known all along.

Our religious faith can be looked at from the outside and analyzed. But such analysis hardly goes far enough. It is hopelessly unable to describe what happens to the feelings. I believe that the healthy Christian has a balance between two different and distinct realms: the truth of God, which informs and guides, and the personal experience of living close to him. In spite of these two, distinct dimensions, our doctrine and how we practice our spiritual life should be complementary. They should be intertwined so that Paul could easily say to us—as he did to the church in Thessalonica in the New Testament, "God chose you, and the means he used was the power of his spirit in your life and your belief in his uncompromising truth" (2 Thessalonians 2:13).

God Calls Us to Balance Our Faith

Through Paul's letter to the Thessalonians, God calls us to balance the spiritual and doctrinal dimensions of life. It was difficult for the church in Thessalonica to grasp this balance. (We can take comfort in knowing that we are not the only ones who may have had trouble with it!) In other parts of the epistle, the apostle Paul complimented the Thessalonians for their faith. They were good people. Paul believed the Holy Spirit led them.

In 2 Thessalonians 2:15, Paul mentions traditions that already existed among the Christians in those early years of the church. These were built on the truth they had been taught, and they probably carried the weight of doctrine as we know it today. The Christians knew what they believed. They were not blown about by every philosophy or theological aberration that passed through town. They looked at religious information objectively.

But the Thessalonians had also developed the ability to look at their faith subjectively. In verses 16 and 17, Paul talks about their love, their hope, and the inner feelings of their souls. He rejoiced in the *balance* in their lives.

Our Lord demonstrated a balance between analytical truth and feelings. In John 1:14 we read that "he came in the flesh and we beheld his glory, full of grace and truth." The combination of those two qualities, grace and truth, is the balance we are considering.

In John 1:17 we encounter that same balance, with those same terms: "For the law was given through Moses. Grace and truth came through Jesus Christ."

When God chooses us to become followers of Christ, he challenges our spirits on the one hand and our minds on the other. Experiencing the two evenly makes our journey into joy exciting. Like Thinker in the story at the beginning of this chapter, we begin to enjoy every mile of the road to our Celestial City.

One Man's Spiritual Journey

Everything I have been saying still focuses on personal experience. You have heard my story, and I have alluded to others in the book. Dan Coffey, a young member of my congregation, is experiencing many of the marks of spirituality we have discussed, and he also has begun to enjoy a remarkable balance between the head and the heart in his life.

I have known Dan for several years. He is a minister's son, and he was trained from his youth "in the fear of the Lord." As a young adult, he taught Sunday school, prayed regularly, and witnessed to unbelievers whenever the occasion presented itself. He knew his Bible and was able to give account of his faith whenever the time was appropriate. In short, Dan looked like a model Christian citizen.

Dan was brought to his knees a couple of years ago. A short-lived marriage to "the girl of his dreams" turned out to be a disaster. His bride left him, his self-confidence was shattered, his faith in God sank to the depths, and all the knowledge he had of Christian doctrine and truth seemed irrelevant. God didn't seem to be listening to his prayers, much less answering them, he thought. Even church attendance became a burden.

Still Dan knew he was a child of God. He struggled to maintain his knowledge of the Lord. He kept coming to church alone.

During a worship service, God became real to him in a personal way. My sermon that particular Sunday was on Paul's conversion on the Damascus road. Paul's experience, of course, focused on a personal encounter with Jesus Christ. As Dan sat there in the pew, he felt God's presence in a special way. His pain and depression melted away as an inner voice seemed to say, "I will be with you."

The final song that particular morning was "I Know Whom I Have Believed." As the congregation sang, Dan not only felt God filling his heart with new strength, but he felt a remarkable peace and joy wrapping itself around him. Tears sprang from his eyes. The same Jesus who appeared to Paul in a flash of light quietly touched Dan.

In the weeks after that encounter, the joy and peace of the Lord remained with Dan. He began to pick up the loose ends of his life. Prayer became much more real to him. It was more than an exercise; it was direct contact with God. Scripture reading became exposure to God's own words.

Today Dan is involved in rehabilitating troubled adolescents. The spiritual dimension of his life has affected his work deeply. Once a week he and a co-worker at his treatment center meet to engage in very specific intercessory prayer and meditation. The two people meet in a quiet room and ask God to heal those with whom they work. While they pray, they visualize the young people, one at a time. They try to picture them in their mind's eye as healthy and healed of the broken relationships or physical problems that brought them to the treatment center.

Often Dan and his friend stop the prayers to go into separate rooms and meditate. When they come back, they share insights they feel the Lord gives them.

Although the two conduct their weekly prayer and meditation sessions quietly, word of what they are doing has begun to circulate in the center. Other staff members say they can see examples of healing taking place in relation to the prayers. Occasionally, Dan says, there will be a report of a dramatic change in a patient, and a staff member will catch his eye and give Dan a knowing smile.

Others in our congregation who know Dan have remarked on the love and peace that seem to radiate from him. The fruits of the Spirit are very evident. Dan has become a blessing to all of us. At this point in his spiritual pilgrimage, Dan has achieved a remarkable balance between the knowledge he possessed from his youth and the spiritual attributes that turned his life around.

The same God who touched Dan stands ready to come into your life. My prayer is that you will embark on your own spiritual adventure.

A Challenge

In the opening of this book, we discussed the Protestant Reformation of Martin Luther and the spiritual reformation within the Church of Spain that was spearheaded by Sister Teresa and Saint John. Luther's Reformation profoundly influenced the Western mind. Even today it affects Christians all over the world. Knowledge of the reformation in Spain is all but lost, but the driving force behind that movement is alive today. Christians still need to feel God.

Winds of change are blowing through many denominations. Spirituality is being discussed, analyzed, and debated. But beyond that, a new understanding of faith changes individual lives.

To some thinkers, the new spirituality seems unsettling. If it becomes an alternative form of Christianity, they perceive it as a threat. If a false dichotomy is set up between the old, mainline religious thinkers and extreme experience-oriented people, then no hope remains for reconciling the two schools of thought.

But if intellectual-analytical Christians will acknowledge a need to augment their solid foundation with some of the beautiful concepts being used by their experiential brothers, they will find their faith much more exciting. It will not be a new form of Christianity—in fact the combination of the two will be as old as the early Christian Church and the Thessalonian Christians who struggled to unify grace and truth.

You and I need this balance in our lives. Our fellow Christians need it, too. Allow me to dream a little. I would like to see more of my compatriots considering the ideas developed by spiritually sensitive Christians. I would like to see groups of believers studying God's Word, listening for his voice, and then testing the messages they receive to confirm their validity. I see seminary students pursuing their traditional courses of study—but also meditating, fasting, loving, and healing. I see solid but stagnant congregations infused with new godly energy. I see bodies of Christians who have had little in common exchange insights and together share God's rich, indwelling love. I see homemakers making time in their busy schedules to draw on God's strength and love—and then they pass that love on to their families. I see children in Christian homes learning basic spiritual truths about love, joy, prayer, meditation, and solitude, and as they grow up they feel at ease practicing these disciplines.

So many good things could happen throughout the world as we Christians learn to balance feelings with intellect. God has given us much, and we in turn have much to give others. The song "Joy to the World" is familiar to all of us, but hidden in the fourth verse of that song we find a sentiment that shows how powerful this all can be:

> He rules the world with truth and grace
> And makes the nations prove
> The glories of His righteousness,
> And wonders of His love.

Study Questions

1. Prayerfully review the questions on your spiritual walk. Can you see room for growth here? What could you do about it?
2. Why is balance important in the Christian's personal walk? What influence could this have on the church? the world?
3. What were the two reformations of the sixteenth century? Which has been more dominant in your life? What steps can you take to bring about a better balance?
4. How did Luther's Reformation attempt to achieve balance? What were the results? How did Sister Teresa's reformation do the same thing? What happened? (Refer to the Introduction if necessary.)